T▲MEOLOGY

Dr. Greco —
THANKS FOR
YOUR SIGNIFICANCE
IN MY LIFE!
- BEST,
Matt

D1275055

GAINING PERSPECTIVE
AND LIVING *YOUR* LIFE
TO THE FULLEST

MATT MUNSON

*To my daughter Kaylee and sons Hunter and Christian –
while it is not quite the bedtime reading you enjoy right now,
know that this book was written with your lives in mind.*

*To my wife, Melanie –
Thank you for encouraging me to live my life to the fullest.*

CONTENTS

PREFACE

"Why"

I was done writing this book.

Truly.

I had gone through numerous iterations, revisions, edits, and rounds of external feedback. The book had reached a point where the feedback I was receiving confirmed that the message I wanted to convey was coming across. And more importantly, it represented the best work I could do. As a result, I was happy. And frankly, I felt relieved for it to be mostly behind me. All that was left was the final artwork, formatting, and hitting "print".

But then a friend of mine said I should check out a TED talk by Simon Sinek relating to leadership. He said it had over 20 million views and might add a language I could reference or incorporate in my book to add value for you, my reader. So I checked it out and was blown away.

Frankly, his concepts of "WHY," "HOW," "WHAT" were not new to me. In fact, I had a boss and mentor who explained to me back in 2005 the importance of these questions. "Matt," he would say, "you must always ask yourself 'WHAT IT IS? HOW IT WORKS?' And most importantly, 'WHY?' " We even had departmental SOPs (Standard Operating Procedures) that answered the "WHAT, HOW, WHY" questions for each process.

Yet Sinek revolutionized it by changing the order of the questions. And in so doing, his concept of "Start with Why" — which is also the name of his book — gave new meaning to asking that fundamental question about core beliefs.

The power of it was impossible to ignore. Through the examples of his TED talk and his subsequent book, Sinek utilized corporations and leaders to illustrate the importance of understanding why we do things. One of the paramount takeaways from the work is that we, as consumers, buy the "why" of companies, not the "how" or "what". Translation, why a company does the things it does matters as much or perhaps even more than the final product and service or its price.

The implications for business were obvious and immediate. Yet I saw an opportunity as it related to the book I was about to release which was more focused on us as individuals. If a corporation clarifying their "why" made such a big difference in what we as people consumed, imagine what the clarifying of our "why" as individuals could do in our own lives.

The linkage was instant in my mind. Sinek's expansion on the meaning of the simple word "why" in the business context provided a succinct vocabulary I could offer you, my reader, as a potential destination for the framework I had already built. Said differently, if I could encourage you to pursue your "why" through gaining perspective in the framework I was offering, you would have the clarity from which to live your life to the fullest. After all, by the pure virtue of reading a book like this in the first place, you are probably pre-disposed to having heard or finding value in Sinek's work. And so, in the true spirit of trying to build upon the collective knowledge that is out there, I had no choice but to go back and incorporate the "why" language into the book.

So, while I was not excited about reopening what was once a finished product in my mind, I felt it was the right decision. And it is funny how life can sometimes offer us confirmations or exclamation points on such decisions. On the specific morning I started the effort of going back and incorporating the why language, having recently signed up for a daily quote from his site, the one I received that day was particularly relevant:

"It's OK if others take our ideas as long as they build upon them. It's called progress." — Simon Sinek

Specifically, *TIMEOLOGY* focuses on the bigger context into which Sinek's and other leadership experts and thought leaders are contributing — trading our time in an effort to live life to the fullest. Ultimately, that is what life is all about — living it fully. And time is of the essence.

But like so many others, I struggled to have a clear "why" for many years. And in the journey to do something about it, I discovered a framework — one that can be used to live life to the fullest — that leads to answering your "why" (though I didn't know at the time that "why" would be that name given to such. Thank you, Simon!)

Gaining Perspective

Through gaining perspective, I have realized a framework for approaching and making decisions in life. This perspective has been further confirmed for me in recent years by simultaneously serving in capacities as both an industry practitioner (CFO) and in academia (as a college professor) where I have received feedback and affirmation of its value from mentors, colleagues, employees, and students. It has been sharpened and refined through these experiences and is ready to be shared with you.

Perspective has come in the recognition that:

1. Time is of the essence. Life is fundamentally about how we trade our time. We need to make sure we are trading it wisely.
2. Our field of play is the world. We need to know what we are dealing with, recognize it for what it is, good and bad, and be able to make good decisions in the face of countless alternatives.

3. We need to know who we really are so we can have an authentic interaction with the world, rather than the other way around.

4. While we often give it different names, what we are actually chasing in life is not just success (what we get) but also significance (what we give) because it is what provides for meaning in our lives. And it starts with incorporating the needs of others into the things we do.

In fact, *TIMEOLOGY* lines up nicely with the "megaphone" metaphor in Sinek's "Start with Why" which I would draw as follows:

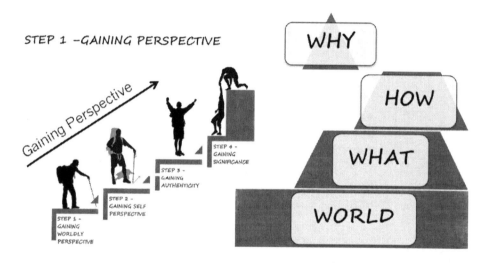

In essence, *TIMEOLOGY* is a climb that gives us the altitude needed to gain clarity on our life. Just as we can see much farther from the top of the mountain than at the base, obtaining altitude in our lives allows for a similar clarity of view. By gaining perspective, we can align our lives to live authentically to who we are and significantly for others. Simply stated, by gaining perspective, we can live our lives to the fullest.

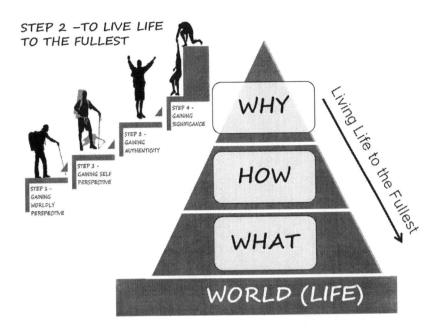

Using this framework, my life makes sense in a way it didn't for years. I have been able to discern what to say yes to and what to say no to. I have gained clarity on the meaning tied to the things I do every day in the various roles I play as husband, dad, son, manager, professor, and so on. I have been able to focus on the things that matter, and eliminate the things that don't. And while my schedule is more filled than ever, the by-product has been both happiness as well as a sense of sustained clarity, empowerment, peace, joy, contentment, and meaning from knowing I am living my life in the fullest way I know how.

That is the essence of this book. It is one of the "what's" inspired by my "why" which is <u>to seek and share knowledge and encouragement so that others can live their life to the fullest</u>.

In so doing, I am living my life to the fullest. By so doing, my hope is you can do the same.

INTRODUCTION

"The Need for Perspective"

1 LIVING LIFE TO THE FULLEST

If I could hear your thoughts, or make your internal dialogue audible somehow, would I hear you asking any of these questions?

"Why are there so many expectations placed on me? How do I know how to respond? Why do I often resent all the demands on my time? School? Work? Family? Friends? After all, didn't I sign up for them? And really, what would I do instead anyway? Is there more to life than just going through these motions? At times it seems so empty. I'm having fun. I'm achieving things. But there has to be more right? Why is it I am so busy all the time and yet feel unfulfilled? Am I wrong for feeling like my time is being taken away from me? Why do I feel like I am wasting days, weeks, months, or even years, worrying about things I cannot control? Why do I trade my time for the highest economic gain? Is that the right way to find the success and happiness I seek in life? Why, when I work so hard on some fronts, do I feel like I am failing on other fronts? For example, the harder I work on the school or career front, the less time I have with family and friends. Or for myself. This seems to create a mutually exclusive relationship where success in one means failure in another. Is that right or is there another way? How

3

do I address it? What is the right path for me to take in life? How do I know? The possibilities seem endless yet I have fear and anxiety about having to focus on one path which means letting go of all others? Yet it's exhausting to keep the doors of opportunity perpetually propped open. What do I do? When I was a kid, life seemed so easy. So simple. Things just fell into place. It seemed natural. Why is it so different now?"

These questions were part of an internal dialogue I had been having for years. One that I struggled to give a name until I read the below quote which summarized it perfectly:

"I believe that it is not dying that people are afraid of. Something else. Something more unsettling and more tragic than dying frightens us. We're afraid of never having lived. Of coming to the end of our days with the sense that we were never really alive. That we never figured out what life was for."

— Harold Kushner

That was it! I was afraid of never having lived. I wanted to soak up life. To experience all of it. To squeeze every ounce of emotion, opportunity, impact, meaning, friendship, achievement, and so forth out of the time that I had on this Earth. I was all in. I was excited. I was motivated and ready to go. It was my time.

Yet there was simply too much of everything. Too many possibilities of things to do or pursue. Too many opinions on what living life should look like. Too many decisions that seemingly required immediate answers. Too many experts saying that the secret to life is this or that. Simply stated, there was just too much noise. And I was overwhelmed.

If you can relate to any of this, you are not alone. Many of us desire a clear direction to pursue in life — a direction that will lead to making fulfilling decisions. Decisions that result in sustained happiness, peace, joy, contentment, meaning, accomplishment, achievement, and so on. Decisions that result in success in life, including the realization of our hopes and dreams.

In short, we desire clarity on how to live life to the fullest.

2 TIMEOLOGY

The struggle to live life to the fullest is bound by time. Time is of the essence, which is to say, that it is really important. Harvey MacKay, a businessman and New York Times best-selling author, says it this way:

"Time is free, but it's priceless. You can't own it, but you can use it. You can't keep it, but you can spend it. Once you've lost it you can never get it back."

In other words, we trade our time to live our lives. Our lives are the cumulative representation of what we have traded our time for. Thus, it follows that we must make good decisions when trading our time. In the game of living life to the fullest, it's about time.

Sports offer a great example of the concept of "trading time". Being a huge football fan, allow me to use one of the best games I have ever seen, to illustrate my point.

It was December 1998 and the Denver Broncos were 12-0 and defending Super Bowl champions. No NFL team had gone undefeated since the 1972 Miami Dolphins and as the Broncos approached the final quarter of their season with a perfect record, discussion started to swirl about whether they could pull it off.

While the Broncos enjoyed future Hall-of-Famer John Elway at quarterback, they had a fourth-year running back in Terrell Davis who was the main catalyst for their success. In fact, he was racing toward becoming only the fourth running back to gain 2000 yards in a single season in the history of the NFL. Thus, the Broncos had become a "run first" team that did not have to rely on the 38-year-old John Elway nearly as much as they had in years gone by.

For the Broncos to pull off the undefeated season, they would have to win four more regular season games starting with their arch rival, the Kansas City Chiefs, who were in Denver for that weekend's game.

The Chiefs, despite being outmatched on paper, wanted nothing more than to be the team to spoil their arch-rivals opportunity at history. And midway through the fourth quarter, the Chiefs had the Broncos on the ropes. In fact, with just about half of the fourth quarter already gone, the Broncos were down 31–21 and time was running out on their bid for the perfect season.

What makes sports interesting is the element of time. If there was not a fixed amount of time, then the teams would continue to exchange the lead, back and forth, without consequence. But what makes the game meaningful is that players are given 60 minutes and the team with the most points at the end, wins.

Thus, there is a lot of planning and strategy that goes into the game, especially as the amount of time remaining in the game starts to diminish. When a team is trailing by 10 points in the fourth quarter as the Broncos were, they have to try to conserve as much time as possible. They use their timeouts so they can stop the clock. They change their offensive strategy to try to pass the ball since it gives them the chance to pick up more yardage with the usage of less time (and incomplete passes stop the clock altogether).

In other words, despite having the best running back in the league that year, because the Broncos found themselves down by 10 points in the fourth quarter, they had to change their strategy to deal with the circumstances they were facing at that moment. As there was time left on the clock, the outcome of the game could be changed. And in this case, it was.

The Broncos came back to score two fourth-quarter touchdowns and win the game by a final score of 35–31 to continue their undefeated season and improve their record to 13–0. (They lost the following week to the New York Giants to end their chance at the perfect season.)

My point is this — if a simple game of football treats time with such value as to use timeouts and change their strategy to deal with it, what does that say about how we might want to treat time in our own lives?

Here are the facts on time:

Fact #1 — Time is limited to 24 hours in a day. Whether you are rich or poor, old or young, girl or boy, smart or not, tall or short, you only get 24 hours in a day.

Fact #2 — You don't know how many days you will have in your lifetime.

Fact #3 — Time is the currency you trade for living life. Your ability to live life is limited by one un-renewable resource — time.

Fact #4 — The choices you make with the trading of your time define how you experience your life — what you achieve, who you develop friendships with, what impact you make, and so forth.

Perhaps Henry David Thoreau said it best: *"The price of anything is the amount of life you exchange for it."*

Since time is so valuable, it follows that the choices we make with trading time determine whether we experience life to the fullest. Unfortunately, many of us do not know what to trade our time for that will lead to living life to the fullest. After all, living life to the fullest is such an abstract thing that it's hard to relate it to specific day-to-day decision making.

In a nutshell, *TIMEOLOGY* is the key to bridging this gap.

If the suffix "-ology" refers to "the study of", it would be appropriate for us to call the endeavor of exploring how we trade our time *TIMEOLOGY*. But *TIMEOLOGY* is much more than simply taking inventory of what we spend our time on.

TIMEOLOGY is a framework by which we can link the inventory of "how we spend our time" with the seemingly abstract "living our life to the fullest." In this way, *TIMEOLOGY* is the perspective that relates how we trade our time, in the day to day decisions we make, with living our lives fully as an outcome. It offers us insight into what takes us from where we are today to where we end up.

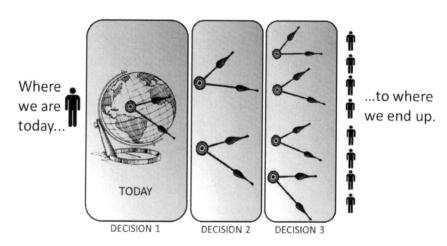

Where we are today... TODAY ...to where we end up.

DECISION 1   DECISION 2   DECISION 3

Even more succinctly, *TIMEOLOGY* is taking action to trade our time to intentionally live our lives to the fullest. And each of us is always on the clock.

3 A SEDUCTIVE WORLD

To further complicate the matter, the world in which we live can be seductive – offering paths that appear to lead to living life to the fullest when in fact they do not.

The first example comes in the number of options available to us. It is said that we as human beings make thousands of decisions each day. And while some are clearly much more impactful on whether we live our life to the fullest, the sheer number is daunting. How do we know if we are making the right ones? Which are the ones to focus on? With that many decisions to make, do we even have the time to stop and think them through?

The world is also filled with opportunities for abundance and consumption. Popular culture offers the idea that by achieving material success, we are able to buy happiness, peace, joy, contentment, and meaning in our lives through the acquisition and use of more things. And therefore, we can live life to the fullest by simply buying it.

Yet another example that has gained momentum lately comes in the form of achievement. The world is honoring the pursuit of achievement through busyness as a badge of success. Achieve this. Juggle that. How many things can I fill my day, week, life, trophy case or resume with? Can I do more than my neighbor? And with the proliferation of technology and social media providing increased ease of comparing our lives to others, fuel is being added to this fire.

One final example could be termed "surrogate-living". The world offers countless forums to emulate life through attaching our identity to the lives of other things. Whether they are characters in our favorite TV program, video game, or even things like "fantasy football" or our business, in some cases we are garnering more of a sense of meaning from surrogate lives than from our own.

These competing priorities and complicating factors present possible detours that can have a large impact on our lives. In fact I would offer this warning – if we don't answer what living life to the fullest is for ourselves, the world will attempt to answer it for us.

Perhaps one of my favorite authors, Hal Urban said it best:

"We can let the media tell us what's important or we can decide ourselves."

Let me give you a personal example that ties these points together.

I will never forget being in the back of a limo bus with the executive team of the Fortune 500 conglomerate I worked for. We were in Shanghai, China and had just completed an executive committee meeting where I, an upstart 25 year old, had the opportunity to present on a strategic project I was managing. I was at least a decade younger than the next youngest attendee and felt honored to be included in what I felt was a very successful group of individuals.

Our CEO was also in attendance. He was wildly successful by all measures: Seven- figure compensation plan; corporate jet waiting to fly him around the world to manage the company; assistants and support staff to tend to his needs so he could focus on providing wealth to the shareholders; responsible for 30,000-plus employees globally; knew top US government officials on a first-name basis; rubbed elbows with captains of industry. By just about any observable measure, he was successful. Clearly he must be living life to the fullest.

Being a recent college graduate who majored in business and finance, he embodied what I had built up and viewed as success. And in many ways, he represented where I desired to go in my career. Just think of what you could do and accomplish with a position like that right?

While private jets and significant compensation plans are great to talk about, these huge economic gains came with significant demands on his time. In fact, the demands were extreme. He was trading virtually all of his time to run this company and all that came with it. (As an aside, it's interesting how the first thing we think about when viewing someone from the outside is usually the great financial windfalls and perks of their circumstance rather than the time commitment.)

On our way to dinner that evening, chance would have it that we sat next to each other in the back of the chartered bus. He started to ask a few questions about my background, my time with the company, and so on. In return, I started to ask him questions about his role, how he liked it, and what it was like.

After a few minutes of conversation focused exclusively on business, I asked about his family. While I am paraphrasing here, my recollection of the response included the following:

1. Well...I had a wife and kids.
2. I worked so much that my marriage failed.
3. During that time, my kids grew up, started their own lives, and because I wasn't part of their lives then, I don't really fit into their lives now.

4. I was a great provider but was gone too much as a husband and father.

Bam! With this one exchange, he blew up my concept of success. Up until that point, I thought that success always brought feelings of achievement, contentment, peace, and joy. And seriously, if anyone had something to be happy about, it would be this man with all the abundance and consumption, all the achievement, and all the power he had at his disposal right? Surely this was living life to the fullest.

Yet I saw in that conversation the huge price that he paid for trading his time in the manner he did. And while I did not probe further, I wonder if he had it to do all over again, given the perspective of how the story played out, if he might have made different decisions.

Now, in fairness, this man was very significant to numerous people. It can be argued very factually that his gifts in business protected and grew jobs from which tens of thousands provided for their families — including me. This is significant to be sure.

But I wonder if he would say he was living life to the fullest. More specifically, was being a captain of industry authentically him? If so, might it raise the question of whether he would have a family if he had it to do over again — especially given the significant time he needed to spend in business?

My point in sharing this example is not to pass judgment on this individual or his circumstances. I know little of him and even if I knew more, the whole point of this book is not about me or any outsider judging whether someone else is living life to the fullest or not. Rather, it is about offering a framework that leads to a perspective from which that person can draw that conclusion for themselves.

From my observations, it appeared that there may be regret or remorse in this individual. That perhaps he did not know consciously the price he might pay for accepting the path he did when he accepted it. What if the world lured him into it saying, "Yeah, go for the CEO role, you have the ability to" and so he did, simply because society had charted that course and he accepted it? That is a far different situation than if he had selected it intentionally because it was authentic to who he was and wanted to be.

While I do not know the road that led him there, I will tell you that that conversation that night in Shanghai, China had a profound impact on my life. And for that I will always be grateful. For the first time in my life, I started to see cracks in the armor of success as I had imagined it and as I had been pursuing it. It created cause for calling a "time out" and reassessing. It did not appear to be as simple as achieving personal highs and acquiring power, fame, and wealth as many of the paths of the world I had accepted seemed to insinuate — there was more to the story. And I wanted to figure it out, especially since the path I currently desired was leading me to follow in the general direction of the CEO.

In looking back now, with the distance and experience of well over a decade, coupled with the benefit of mentors and others who have broadened my view, I have come to the conclusion that there are at least three potential problems that accompany looking to the world for cues on how to live life to the fullest.

First, the world attempts to tell us what success is rather than asking us what we value and who we are to determine authentic success for ourselves. For example, the world tells us that climbing to the top rung of the ladder is success. Therefore, the CEO position is success. The world does not stop to ask if the trade-offs of time with family in exchange for the material gain and achievement are the success we desire.

Second, the world attempts to tell us that doing everything is success. Everyone wants something from us — as consumers, employees, managers, and so on. But because busyness is primarily about things we do or consume, they are temporary by nature. Meaning, the happiness such actions bring is also short-lived — unless of course you keep on the exhausting treadmill by perpetually doing them.

Finally, the world offers mass traveled paths that are like highways, made for the travel of many. Meaning, they don't tie off to any higher theme or meaning in our lives because they aren't based upon "us" the individual, they are based upon "us" the collective. This leaves the act of traveling these various paths impersonal, disjointed and lacking a connection to living our individual lives fully.

So if the world does not have the answers on how to live life to the fullest — yet it is our field of play (i.e., where we live our lives) — how do we trade time for life fully alive? The answer rests in a gaining of perspective.

4 GAINING PERSPECTIVE

It was the summer of 2003 and despite living in California all of my life, I had never been to Yosemite National Park. My girlfriend (now wife) and her family loved going to Yosemite and we had decided to do a trip up for a long weekend.

The big event was a hike to the top of Half Dome, the iconic granite ledge that literally looks like it was cut in half. The distance from the valley floor to the top of the dome is approximately 8.5 miles each way so it was going to be quite a trek, culminating in a climb up the back side of the dome where you use cables to assist your final few yards up to the very top.

The key to hiking a distance like that is to go at a speed that is natural to you. You actually exert less wasted energy going at your pace versus a pace that is too fast or too slow. (Note the interesting parallel to life.)

Thus, while we generally went in groups, we did break up into different subsets of those groups based upon the pace we all felt comfortable with. Being in my mid-twenties at the time, I recall getting into a nice groove and reaching the top of the dome by late morning with two other guys in our party.

Slightly tired but elated by the time I arrived at the top, the view was truly incredible. You could see everything from there. Perhaps the most interesting view was being able to look down on the valley floor where we had started that morning. Wow it looked different from here. You could clearly see the path we had taken to get here. And the obstacles and inclines looked much smaller and insignificant than when we had encountered them.

After enjoying the view for about fifteen minutes, one of my fellow hikers offered to take a picture of me sitting on the ledge. Of all the various pictures capturing moments of my life, the one on top of Half Dome is one of my absolute favorites. Every time I see that picture, I immediately recall what the view was like all those years ago. I am immediately reminded of how different the path we had taken looked from the top of the dome versus when we were on it. And most of all, I recall the peace that came with the perspective that that vantage point provided. There was something about being able to get above it all and have open space that provided peace in what was an otherwise challenging and strenuous trek. Due to the vantage point, things were more clear and the obstacles we had to address were smaller and more manageable because they were part of seeing a bigger picture.

Gaining perspective in your life works much the same way. It provides you a bigger picture of your life. You can actually see your path. Like my hike up to the top of Half Dome, life is full of decisions that represent forks in the road. Do you take the path on the right or the left? Based upon what? If you have the bigger picture and the ability to look down on it, you can see much more clearly where each of the paths lead and decide accordingly. This is the power of gaining perspective.

When you get advice that you should go left rather than right because it is more direct even though it is less scenic, you can pause, consider it, and then validate it against your gained perspective to determine if the recommendation you received makes sense for you. Were you out to try to get somewhere fast or for a leisurely stroll to take in the beauty of the outdoors? The advice is only useful to you in the context of understanding your bigger picture. This is the power of gaining perspective.

Or how about the age old example of the guy who will not stop and ask for directions? In essence, all that is needed is a little perspective, a bigger picture, to determine how to best get to the destination that they already know they want to reach. This too is the power of gaining perspective.

In summary, perspective provides you a context from which to determine how to get from where you are to where you want to go (or help with identifying that). It can provide a foundation for determining if things fit. It can provide a backdrop or guiding principles from which to make decisions. It can help you to see when you are out of alignment. It even offers you a litmus test on what things really are and are not. In short, perspective offers the ability to see life differently than when you are right in the midst of it, by intentionally getting above it and carving out space to see things in a bigger picture.

Gaining perspective is the foundation of this book because it is the vantage point needed to live life to the fullest. So what does it look like? There are four steps to gaining perspective.

THE FOUR STEPS TO GAINING PERSPECTIVE

STEP 4 –
GAINING
SIGNIFICANCE

STEP 3 –
GAINING
AUTHENTICITY

STEP 2 –
GAINING SELF
PERSPECTIVE

STEP 1 –
GAINING
WORLDLY
PERSPECTIVE

1.   First, you must gain "Worldly Perspective". Since the World is where life is lived, it begs the question of "what do you do?"   I am not talking about a job, though that may be part of it, but more specifically, what are all the things (or roles) you do (or play) in life? (ie. friend, father, mother, son, daughter, brother, sister, teacher, scientist, etc, etc) Since we know the world can be seductive and our lives have Competing Priorities and Complicating Factors, it will be important that you identify what roles you play in life, and what opportunities life may present for you to live life fully.

2.   Second, you must gain "Self-Perspective". In other words, you must be able to answer the question — "who are you, really?"   You are unique and there are specific opportunities in the world perfectly suited for you. Knowing who you truly are and want to be is the key to finding them.

3. <u>Third, you must gain an authentic interaction with the world</u>, which is to say, you must impose who you are on the world in which you live. True success is living consistently with who we really are. Therefore, you must be able to answer the question "Is what you do an authentic representation of who you are?" If not, you must identify agreements you have made that stand in the way and utilize tools to prioritize your time, create balance, and build habits/routines to promote authentic living.

4. <u>Finally, you must gain significance</u> by pursuing what can't be taken away. In other words, "Will what you do last beyond you?" Only through including the needs of others in your life do you realize the meaning that leads to the joy, peace, and contentment you ultimately seek.

Through these four steps of gaining perspective, you are able to trade time for the things that really matter — for living your life to the fullest.

You might ask, "Why do we need to go through a four-step framework to be able to make the right decisions that lead to living life to the fullest?" "Why can't I just make the decisions that feel right at the time?"

The answer is you can. But you should be conscious of a convergence of a number of factors that influence where those decisions lead you if you don't have proper perspective. In fact, it has been both my observation and personal experience that these factors make living life to the fullest more challenging than ever before.

For starters, we have more choices and alternatives now than ever before. This concept is covered in American psychologist Barry Schwartz book "The Paradox of Choice — Why More is Less" where he states: "Autonomy and Freedom of choice are critical to our well being, and choice is critical to freedom and autonomy. Nonetheless, though modern Americans have more choice than any group of people ever has before, and thus, presumably, more freedom and autonomy, we don't seem to be benefiting from it psychologically." While having more choices available brings more freedom, it means we are more challenged to try to focus on the things that really matter. Each choice requires a yes or a no decision on whether you will trade your time for it.

Often times, without a larger context to help us make such decisions, we can rely on how we are feeling in the moment to make the decision. And while our feelings are important, they are not necessarily the best guide to making decisions in the moment that add up to pursuing life to the fullest. Take the simple example of ice cream. Eating ice cream in the moment is good. It gives a good feeling. But if your objective is to run a marathon, you cannot afford to give in to the feeling each day while you are training for that marathon. Thus, the larger context helps give "perspective" to the day-to-day decisions that help you pursue your life to the fullest. In other words, having a framework of perspective helps quickly navigate the sheer number of choices and reduce the anxiety that Schwartz referred to.

In fact, here is an over simplified graphic that helps illustrate the difference between a life path without perspective versus one with perspective. If each arrow represents a decision, having perspective gives the ability for the path to be much more focused because of the clarity that perspective has brought about. You are able to make decisions that are in alignment with living your life to the fullest (because you know what that looks like). This allows you to live what I refer to as a "Life of Exclamation".

By contrast, without the benefit of perspective, the feelings of the moment are the factor on which most decisions are made. Each decision is fairly independent and does not tie off to a larger context. The result is a path of U-turns, changes of direction, and a life filled with unanswered questions. This is a "Life of Unanswered Questions."

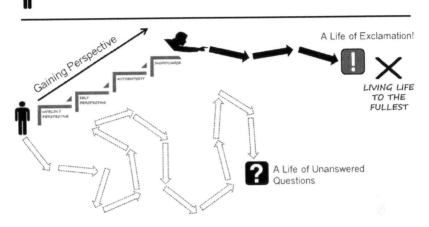

In many ways, this freedom of choice that Schwartz' refers to has come with an overload of information. Even well-meaning information is hard to sort through. I have had many mentors that offered great advice to me personally. I have read countless books on leadership, self-improvement, stories of inspiration and sports heroes with great attributes, and so forth. I have been in the audience for numerous motivational and inspiring speeches that made me want to get up and take on the world. Yet despite the inherent wisdom, subject matter expertise, or lessons from all of these forums, the one thing they all had in common for me was that I had struggled to translate the main takeaway into a meaningful and sustainable action that would help me live my life to the fullest. Why? Because I did not have a larger context for my own life with which to place their message. As a result, I would aimlessly find myself taking a "to do" from each forum which added busyness and noise to my life — often in the blind hope that it represented the magic bullet I was seeking.

Which leads into a point mentioned previously — in many ways culture is creating a belief in us that busyness is synonymous with success. This is creating a wave toward saying yes to everything without making progress on much of anything — kind of like the old adage of being "a jack of all trades and master of none". If we attempt to focus on everything, we will be nothing. In fact, this whole premise is the foundation of the Essentialism movement by author and speaker Greg McKeown. His book by the same title offers great subject matter expertise and encouragement on how to focus on the essential few things rather than the many. I am a big fan! Yet even if it had come out a decade earlier when I was trying to figure out what living life to the fullest was all about for me, without the gained perspective on what was essential for me, the fantastic content of his work would likely have had far less impact and affirmation value for me than it does reading it now. In fact, I would offer that for my life, gaining perspective fits nicely as a necessary bridge — bringing me from a "Non-essentialist" life (of saying yes to everything) to an "Essentialist" life (where one has the clarity to focus on essential things). Thanks for your encouragement and tools on this Essentialism journey, Greg.

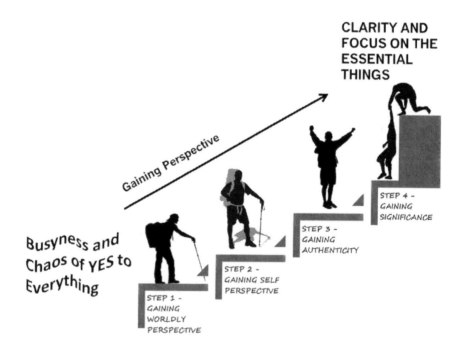

Lastly, marketing and social media are making the adoption of true self-identify for living authentically even more challenging than before. Many of us are pre-disposed to comparing ourselves to others. It is just in our human nature. When we have such easy access to that comparison, we tend to homogenize to fit in rather than to pursue who we really are and embrace what makes us unique. Gaining perspective acts as the anecdote to this by refocusing on who we truly are and imposing that on the world rather than visa versa.

In summary, this is not the first book or thought relating to living life to the fullest (and it won't be the last either). But when compared with much of the conventional wisdom and alternatives presented in the marketplace — and trust me, in my journey to find answers for my own life I have looked high and low — this framework is different for two main reasons.

First, perspective in this book is formed based upon asking you questions rather than telling you the conclusion. In fact, I would contend that perspective is the ability to critically think for ourselves and our lives. By gaining perspective on both who you are and who you want to be, you are able to more accurately determine the opportunities that are authentic to your life. Offering a framework is a far better and more successful approach to living life fully than having an outsider – such as me, who knows nothing about you – try to tell you specific actions that you should adopt for your life.

Second, part of gaining perspective is being reminded of an often glossed over truth that is key to living life to the fullest – life is about what we give, not what we get. Amidst the focus on trying to "fix" ourselves, we become the focus and lose track of the opportunity to use our time to help meet the needs of others. Life is a lot more about what we give than what we get. In fact giving is what leads to the sustained periods of peace, joy, contentment and meaning that we seek. Yet we often forget the path that leads there starts with others and not ourselves.

MOVING FROM "?" TO "!":
BY GAINING PERSPECTIVE

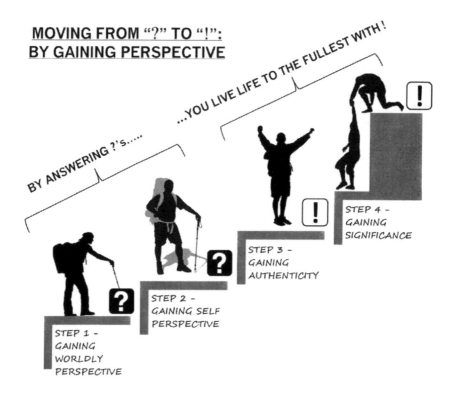

And so, in summary, what I call living authentically and living significantly become the foundation of living fully. Or, said differently, by answering key questions about the world and yourself in steps 1 and 2, you are able to gain the perspective necessary to live life to the fullest through living authentically and significantly in steps 3 and 4. It is how we move from living "A Life of Unanswered Questions" to living "A Life of Exclamation!"

In fact, authenticity and significance are so important that while we will explore them in great detail later in the book, allow me to introduce them to you here.

5 AUTHENTICITY

This morning as I was writing, I had to replace some ink in my printer. Have you ever noticed how expensive ink cartridges are for home printers? So much so that places like Costco have started to do "refills" on ink cartridges for about a third of the cost it might take to buy one new.

If your experience is anything like mine, you have had a bunch of trouble with those "refilled" ink cartridges though. Often times, when I put it back into the printer, it will say something like "Please use an authentic HP Ink Cartridge" and it won't work. Once in a while I might get lucky but in general, I have to use "authentic" HP ink cartridges or else the printer is not quite right.

Isn't that interesting? This simple printer would not fulfill its intended use because it was provided an inauthentic part. Thus it rejected it and did not function until it was provided an authentic part.

It made me wonder — are we that discerning in our own lives? Tell you what, let's come back to that.

Dictionary.com defines the word "authentic" as follows — *"not false or copied; genuine; real; having the origin supported by unquestionable evidence; authenticated; verified."*

Each of us, as human beings, is different. No two are alike. We are individual. We have different interests, passions, skills, talents, dreams, and aspirations. These differences are what make us unique. They are what make the world interesting.

Therefore, what is authentic to me may not be — likely won't be — authentic to you. Let me say that again, what is authentic to me may not be — in fact, it likely won't be — authentic to you.

For example, you may like acting silly and being the life of a party when I am more reserved and shy. For me to act silly, if that is not me, would be inauthentic. Yet, for you to do the same thing, is very much authentic to you.

And certainly, when taking each of us on the whole, meaning all of our interests, passions, skills, talents, dreams, aspirations, thoughts, emotions, and so on, we are all unique. Thus, the only way to be authentic to that uniqueness is take a journey that is uniquely your own in life.

The result is that in the same circumstance, two people who are different may take two different paths. And hopefully, they are doing so while being true to who they really are.

That said, the unfortunate reality is that many of us make decisions that are inauthentic to who we really are. This happens for a number of reasons, which we will explore, but here are just a few:

1. Pressure from family or friends to take a specific course or direction.
2. The "perceived benefits" that await us for taking such a path or making such a decision.

3. Blindly following a "societal on-ramp" because it is the path of least resistance.
4. Not knowing that there is a better, more authentic option.

As a result, we end up "trading time," our most valuable resource in life, for things that don't truly matter to us, or are not consistent with who we really are (if we are being really honest with ourselves). The result? We don't feel fulfilled or fully alive. We feel like we are going through the motions. Yet, we keep doing it, sometimes consciously and sometimes unconsciously.

Authentic living, for the purpose of this book, is being true to who you really are and making decisions and choosing paths in your life consistent with that. And aside from the happiness that such a life brings, there is another compelling reason to consider. We are living in a time where authenticity is at a premium and inauthentic living is being exposed.

Decades ago, it was far easier to present ourselves one way in public and be something else in private. But with our lives being documented by technology moving into so many aspects of our lives, the ability for someone to present such a façade is diminishing.

For example, social media allows us to present ourselves in one way. It memorializes our observations, who we represent ourselves to be, who we associate with, what we like and dislike, and so many other things about who we are.

I recall a story shared by a colleague who worked in the human resources department of a large Fortune 500 company. They were getting ready to make an offer to a candidate for a Vice President position with significant responsibility and six-figure compensation. The candidate, based upon the five rounds of interviews, seemed perfect. But prior to making the offer, the human resources department decided to check out the candidate's social media accounts.

To their surprise, the social media version of the candidate did not reconcile with the candidate they had interviewed. The values that appeared to be demonstrated during the interview process were not the values being demonstrated in the pictures and postings online. It left the human resources department wondering which was the real candidate — the one they had interviewed or the one posted online? Were the online postings just for fun and the appeasement of the pressures of friends and family to "fit in"? Or was that the real person?

Irrespective of the answer, they could not take the chance. They passed on the candidate and ultimately offered the position to a different applicant.

The point is this — in a world where who we present ourselves to be can be reconciled with who we actually are (as captured by modern technology), there is a premium for being authentic. In many ways this is good as we are being held to a higher standard for living an authentic life. But we are far more likely to be "discovered" if we are inauthentic, living one way when in view and another way when not in view.

And aside from the fact that presenting ourselves one way and living another can be exhausting, the more important implications include things like being labeled hypocritical. Or having our ideas and contributions diminished or discarded due to the incongruence in our own lives. Or having regrets for following a path that was not who we really are. Or losing great opportunities like the candidate who was applying to my colleagues' company.

Translation, the importance of living an authentic life is higher than ever. And the importance is only going to grow.

6 SIGNIFICANCE

Many of us are "trading time" in exchange for success, however we perceive it. For some, that means trading significant amounts of time at school to get the best grades possible. For others it means trading significant amounts of time at work to earn the most income or rise in the ranks to better positions. Still others may trade significant amounts of time to accomplish physical feats like climbing a mountain or training to make it as a professional athlete … or raising our families … or… or… or… fill in the blank.

However we view success, the fundamental point is that inherent in the decision to trade our time to pursue such, there is an implication that what we are trading it for must be really important or else why would we trade our valuable time to pursue it?   And thus, it follows that the rewards for achieving such should represent living life to the fullest, right?

Yet, despite finding success in many facets of life, many of us do not find the rewards we thought we would, even once we have achieved success.   Or, at least, do not find them in any sustained way.   True, we might find temporary happiness from getting a great grade in that class we had studied so hard for. We may feel very accomplished for the project we spearheaded at work that landed us the big promotion. We might feel proud of the feat of climbing the mountain we weren't sure we could climb. We even find great satisfaction in our ability to consume when rewarded with financial success. Yet, at the end of the day, the rewards awaiting us at the conclusion of success have one thing in common — they are temporary. Why? Because they are about "getting". "Getting" is a temporary action that is fundamentally about us as individuals. As a result, there is a loneliness that limits it. We are left, after all of this hard work and success, with the realization that perhaps we were after something bigger.

We were right.

By contrast to success, which is about us as individuals achieving or getting, significance is focused on others. While success can bring happiness, the desired benefits of living life to the fullest come in the form of sustained joy, peace, contentment and meaning — all of which result from significance, not success. Therefore, in many ways, significance is the end we actually seek. It's the complementary part that was missing from success.

While we will explore this concept in greater detail, consider the following which Martin Luther King, Jr., summed up perfectly with slightly different words:

"Life's most persistent and urgent question is what are you doing for others."

7 A CALL TO ACTION

Given my experience with the CEO that night in Shanghai, China, I set out on a journey to gain answers in life. If success itself was not the end that would bring the emotions and satisfaction that I thought, then what would? And what was the path to get there? After all, there are so many opinions, how-to guides, books, talks, advertisements, and other inputs offering answers to this question. Which are right? How do we know?

In response, I set out on a journey to try to find a framework into which the wisdom that I would come across during that journey — through and from mentors, speakers, authors, friends, family, coaches, and so on — could fit. A way to piece it all together so that when I felt confused, or lost, or disenchanted, or struggling, I could find my bearings and get back on track.

My findings are captured in this book. Gaining perspective is the key to living life to the fullest and it's based upon two things — living authentically and living significantly.

Through applying this framework in my life, I have found clarity on what is and is not authentic to me. As a result, I have been able to say yes to the things that matter and no to the things that don't. This has led to much personal success.

But perhaps more important, my eyes were opened to the importance of including the needs of others in my life — which is the real end I didn't know I was seeking. This has resulted in a sense of meaning that I did not anticipate or expect to find in my life but was always namelessly looking for.

Therefore, simultaneously living authentically and living significantly is the epitome of living fully. And I look forward to sharing stories and personal examples with you in the pages ahead.

Just as reaffirming as my own experiences with this framework, have been the experiences and feedback of so many of my students. As a college professor, often students will come into office hours to ask questions on some of the accounting and finance material that makes up the content of the undergraduate and graduate classes I teach. Regularly, the conversations will turn to discussion about life, what their next steps will and should be after graduation, and so forth. In many ways this makes perfect sense when I consider their stage in life.

They, like me at that point in my life, have parents that were largely responsible for giving them clarity of purpose in life. Our why, how, and what is pretty well defined as a kid by the wishes of our parents or those responsible for our care.

But in college (or when leaving home), many of us move beyond our parents for the first time. These newfound freedoms allow us to chart our own why, how and whats — if we choose to do so.

For some of my college students, there is great clarity around this achieved during their time in college. They take full advantage of the opportunity college represents to explore and find themselves and leave with great perspective on what living life to the fullest looks like for them.

But for most, including myself at that point in my life, things were not so clear. Many times students ask me questions like, "Should I take this job?" or "What career or industry do you think I should pursue?" Or, even heavier, "How do I find success in life?" or "What should I do next in life?"

On countless pieces of paper, I would draw diagrams and frame the answers to these questions by posing many of the questions and sharing the principles that I finally took the time to memorialize in this book. (I guess now I can say to my students, "Read this!")

You see, when students came to me for advice, I could tell them what to do and, given their lack of experience in life and their perception of my breadth of experience, they would probably be inclined to listen and may even do exactly as I recommend. That is the power that a mentor or advisor can wield.

But what if my advice told them to pursue Path A rather than Path B based upon MY OWN experiences or opinions? This runs the risk of my students living MY decisions in THEIR lives. Since we are different people, this could lead to them following a path that may not be right for them — it may be "inauthentic" to who they are and who they want to be. Yet, because a valued mentor advised them to, they may spend two, three, five, or ten years pursuing such nonetheless.

Thus, rather than tell them what to do, is it not better to offer them a framework to make those decisions for themselves? A perspective they can reach for to help in such situations? The best mentors in my life were the ones who asked the questions and challenged my thinking to help me arrive at my own conclusions rather than giving me their conclusions. They gave the gift of perspective through questioning. They taught me to think critically and take a position. Over time, it developed into a perspective from which to navigate my life. And the best news? It is a perspective that can be re-accessed at any point and any time no matter where we find ourselves in life. Think of it as your personal

"Half-Dome" from which you can gain a view on things at any moment.

The results of this approach have been overwhelming. These students, most of which are experiencing the freedom of decision making in their lives for the first time since being out of the watchful eye of their parents, have provided me a couple of main themes of feedback from implementing this framework in their lives.

First, the framework is resonating with them because it gives a structure to assess who they really are relative to the world in which they are entering. This has been empowering in their ability to develop their own identity as they navigate the opportunities they are quickly coming into contact with. In many cases, I am hearing that there are "questions I did not even know I should ask myself" that, once answered, are empowering them to stand firm in who they are as they assess the paths life is offering. (Moving from question to exclamation in their lives.)

Two, the framework is not limited to the application of career decisions but rather life at large. While they are able to use the perspective to help make career decisions, it has given them a way of relating everything they do to the authenticity test. This is very handy in relationship decisions, religion and faith decisions, and so forth.

Third, being conscious of living significantly has allowed the students to identify opportunities for including the needs of others in what they do — whether it be a career, in the community, or other areas. The result is that it is not a task to check off on a list, but woven in as a part of living a full life.

But whether you are a millennial getting your first taste of self-directed life decision making like my students, a baby-boomer retiring while wondering "now what?" or someone more like me who was well into the responsibilities of life and the "real world" while still grappling with these things, this framework is for you.

In fact, I would go so far as to say that the framework can be applicable to anyone who desires a path to living their life to the fullest, irrespective of age.

Now, there are a few possible outcomes of applying this framework in your life.

One outcome could be that you receive validation that you are already living life to the fullest and simply need to stay the course. This is a fantastic outcome as receiving affirmation of decisions in life helps us to continue moving forward with confidence.

But chances are, if you are reading this, you believe there are areas of opportunity and that this framework can help you adjust. In either circumstance, the benefits include feeling fulfilled, day to day, knowing that you are living your highest and best life, and being authentically you, not who the world would have you be.

Every parent wants their children to have a better life than they did and to learn key lessons earlier on or to avoid making some of the same mistakes. I am no different which is why this quote from Jim Stovall in his book *Wisdom of the Ages* resonates with me:

"Since the beginning of time, humanity developed through the power of collective knowledge. A person isolated from all other human contact will only know what he, himself, experiences. But, when we can pass information along and learn from one another, it is possible to develop more quickly as a society, because each ensuing generation begins with the previous body of knowledge as a base from which to work"

TIMEOLOGY is written in that spirit. It is a framework meant to capture the collective knowledge and experience I have cobbled together in my journey — from countless mentors, coaches, teachers, friends, bosses, students, thought leaders, authors, speakers, pastors and so on — while simultaneously providing a place to fit in the inevitable future contributions you will receive from countless others in your journey.

So whether it is you, Kaylee (my daughter, age 6) or Hunter (my son, age 4) or Christian (my son, age 2) — or you, my students in the classroom — or you, my fellow journeyman or journeywoman in this journey of life — this book is for you. Living your life to the fullest awaits. And it's about time.

PART I:

GAINING WORLDLY PERSPECTIVE

"What are you doing with your life now?"

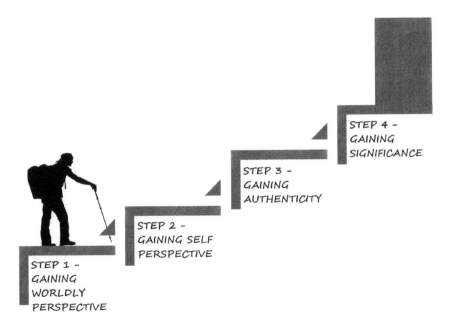

STEP 4 –
GAINING
SIGNIFICANCE

STEP 3 –
GAINING
AUTHENTICITY

STEP 2 –
GAINING SELF
PERSPECTIVE

STEP 1 –
GAINING
WORLDLY
PERSPECTIVE

Do you like movies? I love the movies. They represent an opportunity to get outside of my own life for a few hours and replace it with something different and exciting. I especially enjoy the genres of action/adventure and drama as they tend to have much at stake; "Armageddon" with saving the existence of mankind, the Indiana Jones series with the race of good versus evil, sports stories like "Rudy" where you are cheering for the underdog, and so on. Movies evoke emotion in us and, especially when done properly, stir identification between parts of ourselves and one or more of the characters.

One of my favorite dramas is a movie called "Meet Joe Black" starring Anthony Hopkins and Brad Pitt. It is a story about Hopkins character, a successful businessman who has made his fortune in communications. He is an honorable man, one of values, and takes the responsibility of bringing information and news to people seriously. His life revolves around his two daughters and his business which, as he approaches his 65th birthday, he is considering selling.

The movie really starts when Pitt's character, who is actually the Angel of Death, arrives on the scene to tell Hopkins character that it's "his time" (for dying) and to get his affairs in order. To that end, Pitt starts to accompany Hopkins throughout his day-to-day life as he gets those affairs in order. Pitt goes to the board meetings with Hopkins, has dinner at Hopkins' home with his daughters and their significant others, and a number of other awkward and somewhat comical situations (given all the others in those contexts have no idea who Pitt is or why he is there).

As time passes, Hopkins becomes more ready to face death and it is Pitt who is delaying his original purpose as he becomes more intrigued with life — especially Hopkins' younger daughter who becomes his love interest. As Hopkins continues to put his affairs in order, Pitt continues exploring what the world has to offer, including a funny scene about a simple joy like the taste of peanut butter (something most of us are not intrigued by as an adult).

At the end of the movie, there is a poignant scene that represents the culmination of the movie. (Spoiler alert! Sorry for those of you who may not have seen it. It's been out a long time so if you don't want me to spoil it, stop reading here and go watch it and then come back! Note: It's about 3 hours long.)

Hopkins is celebrating his 65th birthday with a party of stately proportion. After a dance to "What a Wonderful World" with his younger daughter, Hopkins sneaks away to meet Pitt on a hill with a view of the whole party, ready to accept his death. Before walking out of view and away from life, they have a profound exchange.

Hopkins' character, noticing the intensity with which Pitt's character is looking down at the party and the fireworks that are now going off, says: "It's hard to let go isn't it?" referring to the beauty and opportunity represented by life.

Pitt's character, responding to Hopkins after a pause to continue soaking it all in, acknowledges: "Yes, it is Bill."

To which Hopkins' character responds with resounding wisdom and affirmation: "And that's life. What can I tell you?"

In the span of what appeared in the movie to be a few short weeks, the Angel of Death (Pitt), realized the beauty and seductive nature of the world. Despite having a job to carry out with Hopkins, he delayed it where possible to soak in just a little bit more of that beauty and possibility.

But he had an advantage in this movie — he came into the world with a fresh set of eyes, seeing it for the first time (albeit with an adult body). Seeing the possibilities of what it could be and what it had to offer. Yet for many of us, that view has been impacted in some way — positive or negative or both — over time.

So let's start from the beginning.

Think back to your childhood. How would you describe it? As you grew from your earliest memories as a kid to where you are today, how do you view that journey? Was the world beautiful and possible? Is it still? If not, when did it change?

For my part, I had an amazing childhood. I think back on it with such fondness. Perhaps it was the fact that my parents made us kids (I have a younger brother and sister) the epicenter of everything. We always felt loved. We went to church. Were involved in sports. Loved school. Had grandparents that loved to make us the center of their lives too. It was truly a blessed childhood. And the world was an amazing place as a result.

Everything seemed possible. It was a world where you still played "hide and go seek" and thought that if you stood still enough, even though you were in plain sight, no one would find you. It was a world where getting candy in your plastic Jack-o-Lantern on Halloween was all it took for your life to be complete. It was a world where a coloring book and a box of 64 Crayola's could leave you happy and content for hours. It was a world where staring at the clouds in the sky, you could clearly see that they were animals and trains and other objects, not just billowy white things blowing by.

Success for me was getting good grades or hitting that key single in the 6th inning to win the little league baseball game. Significance was standing up for the not-so-cool kid on the playground at school or opening the door for an older couple at the store. But frankly, I never thought of the world or anything I spent my time on in such terms. I just lived. It was natural. It was authentic.

But you did not have to have a charmed life like I did as a child to feel this way. My best friend growing up had a different set of circumstances. He had just moved to town. He didn't know many people. In the city where we lived, he was a minority from a cultural standpoint. His parents were divorced. His dad traveled a lot and was not home much. He hardly ever saw his grandparents except when they flew over from Asia for a month or two at a time every year or two.

Yet, despite all that, we both had the same overarching view on childhood. It was amazing. The world was large and it represented a huge playground to explore. Our perception was that companies and people were good and always did the right thing. Life just flowed, and we flowed with it, enjoying every moment and naively thinking it would always be this natural, this authentic.

But third grade turned into fourth, fifth and sixth, and then junior high, then high school and college, and before we knew it, the "choose your own adventure" of life had landed us in the real world. For me, I was now a college graduate and took a job as a financial analyst at a Fortune 500 company. It would seem the possibilities of childhood like being in NASA, or a pro basketball player, or the President of the U.S., were now out of the question.

My world narrowed quickly from endless possibilities to exactly what I was doing in a short period of time. That was a shock. And with that, I lost touch with my imagination and hope.

Remember the disappointment when you found out that Santa Claus, the Easter Bunny, and the Tooth Fairy were not real? For me, the narrowing of the possibilities of life was of this magnitude.

I felt a mourning of dreams that may not come to pass — that while I had never actually done anything specific to pursue a

46

career at NASA, it still seemed possible to me growing up. And it wasn't until I was in that financial analyst chair in my first post-college job that I started to realize those paths may never be travelled in my life. There was something about spending 50 plus hours a week focused on one thing that made the other possibilities in life more distant.

Does this resonate in any way for you? As you look back on your childhood into adulthood, is there a mourning of dreams that may not come to pass? The loss of ____ (fill in the blank). What are those blanks for you in your life?

Perhaps this is the life of an adult, I thought. That such hopes and dreams are meant to be left behind when we "grow up". Perhaps there is a need for us to simply accept this as part of life and move past it. After all, isn't acceptance of reality part of life?

But I am not sure I am ready to give it up that easily. As Hopkins said, "It's hard to let go isn't it?" Yes, it is.

So might it be possible that rather than let go of those hopes and dreams and possibilities, we choose to compensate by filling these holes with the things and paths of this world instead? That we look to the world for affirmation of who we are and what we are doing with our lives? That we replace the possibilities of childhood with ways we can compare our adult lives to others?

For me, as I grew up, some of the attractiveness and endless possibility of the world got replaced with obligations, fears, and competing priorities that were not present when I was a kid. Some would say I became "jaded." But I think I simply grew up.

Things now stood in the way of that natural flow of life that seemed to come so easily as a kid. Things now complicated life and made the path blurry. In an effort to better understand them, let's give these "things" some formal names.

8 LIFE'S INVITATIONS

When you are a kid, you usually have the luxury of just worrying about yourself. It's easier to live in balance because you are only responsible for yourself and probably only partially because you have a parent(s) to look after you. Your "job" might be to go to school and get good grades and try hard at your sports teams and demonstrate good manners. You likely have some chores around the home and some expectations of doing a few things like going to church. Your friendships are pretty easy to maintain because you see them each day at school or on the sports teams on which you play. And family time is fairly easy too because you likely see your immediate family every day and, if you are lucky, perhaps your grandparents and extended family regularly.

Adulthood is different. The world requires many things of adults and extends them in the form of what I call "invitations". I use the term "invitations" because they are actually choices that we are able to make as to whether we accept them or not. For example, have you ever been invited to two things on the same day and had to make a choice on which to go to? Or perhaps you tried to do both by cutting each of them short?

Life is much the same way. We get constant "invitations" from various aspects of our lives we need or desire to have. Frankly the list could be endless, but broadly speaking, invitations arrive in the form of basic needs and optional wants. And we often accept numerous invitations on both fronts both consciously and unconsciously.

Let's start with basic needs. As adults, you are usually fully responsible for your own care (and many times the care of others). This involves many elements, most of which you likely weren't responsible for as a child. You must provide for the basic needs of food, shelter, clothing and so on. This involves needing to do some sort of job or vocation which allows you to earn the resources (money) to meet these needs. Aside from the time that takes, you are actually the one who goes and does the shopping for the food, buys the clothes, and facilitates the necessities of life. This invitation requires time above earning the resources with which to do it. Add on the need to tend to the "administration of life" — like paying the bills and getting your car's oil changed — and you have a considerable amount of time in your life already spoken for.

Immediately following those basic needs are invitations relating to things like your own personal health. Whether you categorize them as basic needs or optional wants, the reality is that they take considerable time. For example, take fitness. While we often don't "work out" as a kid, we usually have to do so as an adult to stay healthy, especially if you spend a disproportionate amount of time in front of a computer (as I do). This invitation requires time. Or how about just finding some down time for you to step back from life or spend a few hours doing something you really like to do? You get the point.

Family and friends provide another invitation in life (I'll leave it to you to debate whether it's a basic need or optional want. It's probably some combination of both). Whereas we were able to see our friends at school growing up, it takes time and intentionality to stay connected to them as we grow older. My dad once said to me, "Matt, if you can find enough true friends to fill up one hand (i.e., 5), you are a truly lucky man." By this measure, I would say I am lucky but would confess that the foundation of the friendships that meet those standards were mostly established prior to adulthood and with a few exceptions, adding newer ones has been a challenge. Why? Because it requires time. Also, as we likely no longer live with our immediate family like we did when we were younger, seeing and catching up with parents, brothers, or sisters is an invitation that requires time as well.

And I have not even got into invitations like education, community, sports, church, recreation, hobbies, and so forth.

My point is that as an adult, there are many basic needs you are tending to that were not present as a kid. Tending to these basic needs requires considerable time with a job or career usually being the biggest culprit. Yet, the reality is that we need to earn money or gain resources to meet these basic needs — and there is usually no way around this.

As a result, we face a challenge as adults that we did not face as kids. Because we are responsible for both the basic needs and optional wants — and because we desire to have both in our lives — we must determine the balance between what we must do (ie; work to provide for our families) and what we desire to do (have meaning in our lives, feel happiness, experience joy, and so forth). Thus, we are faced with the ambiguous question of determining "how much is enough" in each aspect of our lives. More specifically, how do we trade time to balance our basic needs and optional wants so we can live life to the fullest?

9 LIFE'S COMPLICATING FACTORS

To make matters even more challenging, there are Complicating Factors that add more ambiguity.

In my own journey thus far, the single largest obstacle to living life to the fullest has been the impact of society on me personally. And the scary part is, for many years, I did not even know it was happening.

We live in one of the most amazing times in human history. We can be just about anywhere in the world within 24-36 hours given the modes of transportation available. We can communicate with family, friends, or associates all over the world through a host of different mediums (phone, email, text messaging, internet, social sites, blogs, etc). We have information and entertainment at our constant disposal. Technology and research provide cures and treatments for countless diseases. In short, we have the ability to meet most of our needs and wants with virtually instant gratification. Without diving deeper, one could argue that we have an opportunity to realize a quality of life unmatched by generations past. And on many fronts, I would agree.

But inherent in these amazing times are challenges.   Obstacles that come in the form of complicating factors that can lead us down a path that we believe to be our own, only to find it was someone else's.

For me, this started with two realizations: (1) there are more possibilities than ever before and (2) we are more heavily influenced by media and marketing than at any time in history.

Madison Avenue spends billions of dollars a year influencing our minds on what success is and what it is not. From what we wear to what we drive to what we do to what toys we have to what house we live in to what we look like to what our spouse and children look like.   In fact, by the year 2017, it is estimated that US Advertisers will spend close to $200 billion on paid advertising. And for clarity on how big a billion is, if I handed you a $1 bill every second, it would take me almost 32 years to hand you $1 billion.

Be it through consumption of products or services, or achievement of a certain lifestyle, the media offers regular doses of what "success" is.   Here are just a few of the themes:

- Success is Materialism — More is better. "He who dies with the most toys wins."   Being able to buy what you want, when you want, is success.

- Constantly Upgrading — Bigger is better. If you have the 3 Series BMW now, next time you must get the 5 Series.

- Pop Culture — Fame is better. Success is being known and famous. After all, you deserve it.

The media is driven by advertising. Without advertising dollars, the media would largely not exist. Therefore, the programs offered by the media, along with the advertising that is presented on such mediums, usually has a goal of ultimately selling a product or service.

So how does that affect us and what does that have to do with answering the question of "how much is enough"?

Well, advertising campaigns focus on influencing the target audiences' thinking to perceive our own value as being derived from the consumption of that product or service. Simply stated, for us to be successful, we must consume what they are selling.

In this way, that the media and advertisers use programs and campaigns to shape and dictate what success looks like for us — which impacts our perspective. And sadly, many of us, looking to the world to fill that void in our lives, spend years chasing and consuming things thinking that it represents a path to living life to the fullest, myself included. There are many reasons why, but broadly, I would classify them as playing on our "temptations" and "fears". Allow me to share briefly from my own life to illustrate my point.

My educational background is focused in accounting and finance. Thus, I have been trained to do analysis and identify ways to "maximize shareholder wealth" or, in simple terms, to make more money. And my training shows that the financial statements — specifically a balance sheet where it shows your "equity" or "net worth" — provide a scoreboard for success.

The result was I started to make decisions in my life based heavily on maximizing my personal net worth. Why? Well, I viewed money as the ability to have control over things, choices in life, and freedoms. All of these are very attractive. I figured that if I could accumulate wealth (money), that once I figured out my desired basic needs and optional wants, I would have it ready and waiting.

While saving or acquiring money is not fundamentally bad, it was becoming the vantage point for my perspective. When my net worth was up, I was a success. When it was down, I was not. But perhaps more importantly, I started to see money as providing security. It was the currency or resource that I could trade to get what I wanted. And thus, more of my life and the life decisions I was making were being influenced by the impact or contribution they could make to my "money and materialism" temptation.

John Wooden, arguably the greatest basketball coach ever, was once asked what disappoints him most when he looks around America. He replied, *"That's easy. There is simply more emphasis on material things than in the years gone by. I think I see it in business, and I think I see it in the home life."*

Falling into the temptation of Money and Materialism stemmed partially from some fears as well; a fear of boredom and a fear of not having enough. Working hard on the career front helped me avoid boredom. It gave me a real life team to be a part of, just like I had when I was younger in sports. It provided me a challenge and a purpose which are things that my personality desire. It also helped me feel like I was doing something to address my fear of not having enough. This fear that I only have so many good earning years in my life and needed to make the most of it so I could have the resources necessary for the next phase of my life, wherever that would lead. And it probably didn't hurt that I was getting positive attention from teammates and bosses for the work I was doing.

While working hard and saving are not bad things — quite the contrary actually — doing so in this manner was creating an identity for me that was based upon my net worth. Money, as well as the vocation I was using to earn it, were becoming synonymous with who I was. I had no sense of "how much is enough" because my answer to that question was simply the ambiguous "more".

It started to create a nasty cycle that, if perpetuated, could have even more significant impact on things like my marriage, my family and friendships, my health, and the basic needs and optional wants that I knew intellectually were more important. Yet the crazy part was the fear of not having enough, while not rational, was being perpetuated because it was emotional. It was what I had filled my blank with as I went from kid to adult.

I needed perspective on the situation. And fast. (A bit later in the book I will share how I dealt with this issue through the gaining of perspective.)

10 GAINING YOUR WORLDLY PERSPECTIVE

The world is your field of play — it is where you trade time to live your life. While the world is full of amazing life invitations for you to live out and experience, some of those invitations may lead you down the wrong paths and away from living your life to the fullest.

But before you can determine the right paths — which you will do later in the book — you must first identify the various roles or "hats" you wear in life. It's almost like taking inventory of what you are doing right now. For example, I have a number of roles I play in life. I am a son, brother, husband, father, friend, CFO, professor, church member, neighbor, countryman, and so on. At various times in my life, I was also a coach, teammate, and member of a rock band (back in college — those were the days!).

Think about your life. What are the various roles or hats that you wear in life? Here is a simple form that you can fill out so you can reference them later on.

WHAT ARE THE ROLES YOU PLAY IN LIFE?

In addition to knowing the roles you play, there are a few additional pieces of information that will be helpful as you continue in the effort to gain perspective. After all, your objective at this stage is solely to take inventory and gain worldly perspective on how you are currently interacting with the world (i.e. the field of play for life). Later on, you will be able to make adjustments if deemed necessary.

These additional questions have to do with your fears and feelings about the world. Often times, fears can drive a lot of behaviors or choices. Thus, it is important to identify what your fears are, and name them specifically. For example, as I just shared, one of my fears was not having enough financial resources at various stages in life to live the life I desired. This was driving some of my behaviors (ie. working long hours, making all decisions based upon maximizing the monetary outcome, etc). So calling this out as a fear was an important step in me gaining worldly perspective.

Simply indicate your fears in the table provided:

WHAT ARE YOUR FEARS IN LIFE?

Beyond fears, it is also important to name things that you would change about the world. Whether you see them as an opportunity or just want to lodge some complaints against the world for the "way things are," these are extremely valuable to try to call out. One reason is that by identifying the thing(s) you would change about the world, it forces critical thinking in support of not simply accepting things the way they are (which can be one of the major barriers to living life to the fullest). Furthermore, it provides clues on where you may find opportunities to live life to the fullest by being at the front of efforts to change the world for the better (based upon how you see it).

For example, I have always been fascinated with the idea of living life backwards. Just think about it. How cool would life be where we start out our lives with the wisdom we have gained throughout our lifetime? We have all of the financial resources we have acquired from a whole lifetime. And then our bodies get healthier and younger. Aches, pains, and wrinkles go away. Hair gets darker or comes back. We move toward less and less responsibility as we move back from adulthood to childhood. And our view of the world gets simpler again.

Without a doubt, if I could change something about the world, I would have us all live life backwards. But since I don't have the magical powers or pixie dust to make that possible, I will continue to seek the wisdom and lessons of others and my own life to try to achieve some of those benefits (ie. this book).

So what would you change about the world? Simply indicate the things that come to mind in the table provided:

WHAT WOULD YOU CHANGE ABOUT THE WORLD?	
1.	
2.	
3.	
4.	
5.	

The goal of this activity is to simply give names to the things that make up your "world view" so that you are conscious of them. You will refer to them later as you continue to gain perspective.

So, in summary, allow me to net it out for you this way. The world is your field of play. It is where you live your life. Therefore, it is important to know the world is full of endless opportunities and possibilities, many of which can lead to living life fully and many of which will not. Being conscious of this is one step. Making a pact that you do not want to settle for the paths that lead to just going through the motions of life is another key step.

C.S Lewis, from *The Weight of Glory, and Other Addresses*, stated it this way: "We are halfhearted creatures, fooling about with drink and sex and ambition when infinite joy is offered us, like an ignorant child who wants to go on making mud pies in a slum because he cannot imagine what is meant by the offer of a holiday at sea. We are far too easily pleased."

So how do we find the paths that lead to living life to the fullest?

Steve Jobs offers this answer:

"Your time is limited, so don't waste it living someone else's life. Don't be trapped by dogma — which is living with the results of other people's thinking. Don't let the noise of other's opinions drown out your own inner voice. And most important, have the courage to follow your heart and intuition. They somehow already know what you truly want to become. Everything else is secondary."

In other words, the next step is to truly know who you are.

GAINING WORLDLY PERSPECITVE SUMMARY

"WHAT ARE YOU DOING WITH YOUR LIFE NOW?"

Key Points

- The world is where life gets lived.
- It is full of endless opportunity.
- But, if we don't choose the direction of life for ourselves, the world will offer up its own direction for us.

Action Items

- Identify the roles you play in life.
- Identify your fears.
- Identify what you would change about the world if you could.

PART II:

GAINING SELF PERSPECTIVE

"Who are you, really?"

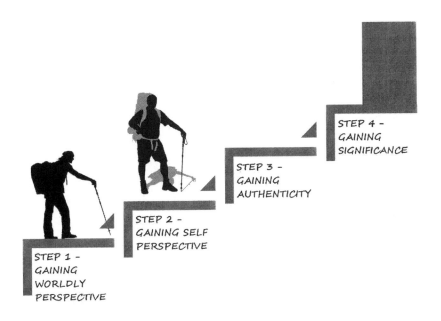

STEP 4 –
GAINING
SIGNIFICANCE

STEP 3 –
GAINING
AUTHENTICITY

STEP 2 –
GAINING SELF
PERSPECTIVE

STEP 1 –
GAINING
WORLDLY
PERSPECTIVE

Have you ever taken something for granted, having never questioned it, since that appears to be the way it has always been?

- Why do croutons come in airtight packages? Aren't they just stale bread to begin with?

- If people from Poland are called Poles, then why aren't people from Holland called Holes?

- Why is a person who plays the piano called a pianist, but a person who drives a race car is not called a racist?

- If it's true that we are here to help others, then what exactly are the others here for?

- What hair color do they put on the driver's licenses of bald men?

- Why do they put pictures of criminals up in the Post Office? What are we supposed to do, write to them? Why don't they just put their pictures on the postage stamps so the mailmen can look for them while they deliver the mail?

- Why do banks charge a fee due to insufficient funds when they already know you're broke?

Yet, when you are asked about these things, you kind of say, "Oh yeah, why is it that way?"

While the above are kind of fun, and have little impact on you living your life fully, these do illustrate the concept of "agreements" that we have simply accepted as norms in our life. I first heard the term "agreements" used for these types of things by author and speaker, John Eldredge. For me, "agreements" have become analogous to anything we accept as norms in our life without really thinking them through or asking "why". While some may have little impact, the reality is that many agreements can have significant impact in our lives. Why? Because they shape our perspective. And we rely on perspective to make the important decisions in our life.

Therefore, the question is, "Have you made any agreements in your life that may be impacting your ability to live authentically to who you are?"

That's a heavy one. Tell you what, let's come back to that question. First let me share a bit more about "agreements."

11 AGREEMENTS

Have you found that in life, we often accept things the way they are rather than asking if that is the way it should be? This acceptance is the fundamental barrier to critical thinking. It is also the fundamental barrier to living an authentic life. For example, why do so many people buy a car? Buy a house? Get a cell phone? Etc?

For many, before there is a need, there is this "societal pathway" with so many people traveling it that in the absence of asking "why?", it seems like the next logical place to go. It's like an interstate highway that is 15 lanes wide; a well-charted and well-travelled path just asking for us to join the millions of others on the same road. After all, there must be a good reason they are all on that path right?

While it may be slightly taboo because I am a college professor, let's explore this concept using the example of going to college (since one day my own children will be crossing the bridge on this very decision).

There is a clear societal pathway that once a student graduates from high school, there is an implied agreement that most should continue on to college. Society has told us things like:

If you want to be successful, go to college.

If you want to get a good job, go to college.

If you want to grow as a person and have a good time (even some partying), go to college.

But college is the key. If you do not go to college, you are not likely to be a success. And your life will suffer as a result. (Side Note: Notice the fear element presented here which ties back to our discussion in Gaining Worldly Perspective.)

The result of this agreement that college is the logical next step in life promotes many students blindly coming to college. It has been my observation that a significant portion of these students have not really thought through how college relates to their desired path in life. They are hoping there is some magical answer awaiting them (or else why would society place such importance on it and so many people do it). Therefore, it was not a conscious decision, but a passive one following that societal pathway or agreement. Let me explain.

There are many students that have a specific purpose or purposes with college. I want to be a pharmacist. Thus, I need to get certain education and knowledge to pursue such. Or, I want to be an athlete and continue my athletic career and college provides me the opportunity to do such. Or even, I am not sure what I want to do with my life so I want to explore numerous different avenues to see what's out there and college provides me the platform to do just that. There are countless different examples, all of which share one thing in common — they were conscious decisions where the question "why" was asked and subsequently answered.

Now, consider the antithesis. I just graduated high school and desire to run and operate my family farm in central California. Or I desire to work in and eventually own an auto-repair station. Or I have never really been interested in formal education and would prefer life experience to determine what my next steps would be. Is college a logical pre-requisite for these desired paths? Especially given the cost of education, is this the right direction to take?

Before dissecting this, allow me a few disclaimers. I am a huge proponent of college and education in general. It has served me very well in my life and I am passionate enough about it to trade my own time to teach in that forum. Despite its significant cost, evidence suggests it is still the best investment most of us make in ourselves and can set the trajectory for much success in life (not only because of the earning potential of those with degrees but the critical thinking and skills that are learned that can be applied to all aspects of life — if done properly). But experience has also shown me college is not for everyone. And the notion that is often implied by the agreement or societal pathway that college is the only path to success is a complete misnomer.

My point in sharing all of this is, in life we have accepted many agreements, mostly unconsciously. For that high school graduate that desires to run the family farm in Central California, college may be a necessary experience because they desire to have the business skills to run the farm. Or perhaps they desire to take food sciences coursework to gain further education on their industry and product offering. Or perhaps they decide against college.

Whatever the conclusion, the reasons behind our decisions in life are the key. Should the high school graduate go to college? The best way to answer this, or any question in life, would be to ask "why" three to five times. Consider this dialogue on the high school graduate who desires to run the family farm:

Why do you want to go to college?

Because I desire to learn business skills to run my family's farm.

Why?

Because skills like accounting, management, marketing, and economics will give me the tools necessary to protect and perpetuate my family's hard work over these multiple generations.

Why?

Because they will broaden my knowledge, assist me with critical thinking and decision-making, and help me to grow to meet this challenge.   I will also learn teamwork and have new social opportunities personally and in business settings that I will grow from.

So is it worth the investment of the time and cost to go to college? Why or why not?

Yes, it is worth it, given the benefits it can provide me in running my family's farm.

While I know this sounds very simple, we would be amazed at how many agreements we have unconsciously accepted in our lives.   Taking the time to ask "why" helps us understand the reasons and rationale for making a decision.

Taking it a step further, I would even suggest that for life's biggest decisions, memorializing our answers to the "why" questions in a way that we can refer back to in the future might even be a good idea. I have done that with big decisions in my life which, years later, I second guessed (ie. buying or selling a home). Having answered the "why" questions and documenting it helped me to recall why I had made those decisions in that moment which resulted in peace later on when I wanted to second-guess them.   It also acts as a get-out-of-REGRET-free card which is a great insurance policy against looking back with remorse.

12 GAINING YOUR SELF PERSPECTIVE

Life is a constant process of self-exploration and understanding. You are unique and there are specific opportunities in the world that are perfectly suited for you. Knowing who you really are is the key to finding them. Said differently, in order for you to live life to the fullest, you must know who you really are. Only then can you determine answers to questions like which path or direction to take in your life.

So, while a simple series of questions will not likely render a huge "ah-ha" moment, these questions and exercises can help to set a backdrop or a context you can use later to test the authenticity of your interaction with the world.

So what questions do you need to answer to gain Self-Perspective? They relate to three key areas for which we are all unique: (1) Dreams and Aspirations, (2) Interests and Passions, and (3) Skills and Talents. Let's start with some easier questions and then move into some harder stuff.

Part 1 — Dreams and Aspirations

First, forget about any preconceived notion you have of the world (as best you can). If it helps, go back to your childhood when you felt everything was possible and were naïve to the ways of the world. Then answer the questions in this table.

PART 1 – DREAMS AND ASPIRATIONS	
QUESTIONS	RESPONSES
What did you dream of doing with your life growing up?	
Have you let go of those dreams? If so, why?	
What is in the way of getting them back?	
Are there any agreements you made that are barriers?	

As I look back on my life, I dreamed of a number of things and also recall some things that clearly were not dreams of mine. For example, I recall my mom and dad taking me to see the movie *Top Gun* when it came out in the theaters. My mom, who always wanted to fly fighter jets, came out of the movie so pumped up and asked me: "Matt, wouldn't it be great to be able to fly one of those planes?" Apparently, though I don't specifically recall saying it, I turned to my parents and responded: "Mom, Dad, if it's all the same to you I think I'll just get a desk job." What eight-year-old kid says that after watching *Top Gun*? (Funny that it turned out that way.)

My point is that some things are clearly roads we don't want to take and knowing that is helpful as it eliminates some of the paths and allows for focus on the others.

That said, there were a number of things I did dream of doing. Unfortunately, upon reflection, I came to discover that I had temporarily let go of a lot of them as I filled my life with the things of this world. For example, my first home was really expensive.

My wife and I were afraid, due to the rapidly increasing prices of homes during that time, that we would never own one unless we jumped in right then (notice another "fear"). And thus, we paid a lot for the home.

It did not occur to me at the time but when we made that decision, we made an agreement. Because we wanted that house, and it came with a significant price tag, we were now tied to certain career paths that were conducive to making the income necessary to support that price tag. And, in so doing, the agreement acted as a barrier to having the time and freedom to pursue some of the dreams I had in life — one of which was going back to get a PhD. and become a college professor. (Due to some other opportunities and the support of some great mentors and bosses, I was lucky to have ultimately had the opportunity to live out this dream.)

Yet this, in its simplest form, is an example of how agreements, unconsciously made over time, pile up to stand in the way of the dreams we once held. Give names to those agreements in your life by completing the table.

Part 2 — Interests and Passions

Life is so busy with "to-dos" that we don't often make it a priority to spend time doing the things that make us most happy. I once heard a saying that I thought captured the essence of this. We need to "find some time to lose track of."

When we as people don't have time to lose track of, we tend to drift further from our own identity, further from our true self. In my own life, I have found this to be true. There were many stretches in life where I would go weeks or months at a time filling every moment with some commitment or responsibility. The more I 'went through the motions', the more I found myself becoming a robot, just administering my life. There was no interest, there was no passion, there was just administration. Just meeting my basic needs and obligations. And even time that used to be "free" — like showing up a few minutes before an appointment — has been filled with looking at my phone.

A critical part of living authentically is re-establishing or getting in touch with those interests and passions. Here are some key questions that will help identify the interests and passions in your life.

PART 2 – INTERESTS AND PASSIONS	
QUESTIONS	RESPONSES
What is it, that when you do it, time seems to fly by?	
When you have free time, you love to ____ ?	
How often do you get to do these things?	
If not very often, what is in the way of getting back to them?	

Take a moment to jot down your answers.

76

Part 3 — Skills and Talents

Each and every one of us has a superior ability to do something well. As a matter of fact, I cannot think of anyone I have ever met who has just one. My point is that everyone has skills and talents. Abilities to do something better than most other people can do that same thing.

Some of the easiest examples come from the sports world. Take Michael Jordan as an example. By all accounts, Michael Jordan possessed the mental strength to focus more intently and for longer periods, than others. Michael Jordan also possessed the physical aptitude of coordination and athletic ability. The combination of his mental advantages and physical abilities represent just two skills and talents that Michael Jordan possessed that were better than most other people who might attempt the same thing. Now, we all know he utilized these skills and talents, along with others, to be the best basketball player of his generation and maybe ever.

But the point I want to underscore is that while these skills and talents are clearly rewarded in the game of basketball, they could also be rewarded in a completely different application as well. Take golf for example. Mental strength and physical coordination are also rewarded in the game of golf where there is a combination of both focus and eye-hand coordination that are required. And while he did it for hobby, this explains why Michael Jordan is a pretty good golfer as well. The point is this: had basketball not been an interest and passion for Michael Jordan, those skills and talents would have been useful when applied to other opportunities in life.

Skills and talents can also be a bit more abstract. Perhaps one of my foremost skills and talents — not that it is that useful — is I can recite just about every line from numerous movies. From the "Code Red" scene in *A Few Good Men* to the "I'm Your Huckleberry" duel in *Tombstone*. My point in sharing this is twofold. One, make sure you don't watch those movies with me — I am that annoying person that will say the lines before they are said on the TV.   Two, don't limit your self-assessment of your skills and talents.   Think of anything and everything that you do comparatively better than most people you know.

PART 3 – SKILLS AND TALENTS	
QUESTIONS	RESPONSES
What are you comparatively better at than others?	
Where do you get to put these skills and talents to use in your life?	
How often do you get to put them to use?	
If not very often, what is in the way of using them more?	

Don't feel bad if it takes you a bit of time to identify some items for this section.   Often times, we are not aware of how good we are at certain things.   So take some time and capture anything that comes to mind.   Or, ask a confidant or trusted friend their observations about your skills and talents if it helps.

13 THE EXPOSE AND THE EPITATH

Having warmed up with gaining self-perspective on dreams and aspirations, interests and passions, and skills and talents, we are ready to get into some heavier stuff. The Exposé and the Epitaph may be the most revealing and profound self-perspective exercise you have ever done. But, done right, the perspective you gain from completing it honestly is pure gold.

Have you ever seen an older picture or heard a song, and it immediately took you back to a specific place and time in your life? And as you reflected on it, were you amazed at how much different you are now versus back then? Pictures or songs or even places or smells can immediately take us back to times gone by, to remember who we were, and have the opportunity to compare it to who we are today.

But perhaps an even more valuable comparison would be if we had the benefit of seeing the picture of us today compared to a future picture of ourselves. What would that difference be? The exercise of the "Exposé" and the "Epitaph" is an extreme version of such a comparison.

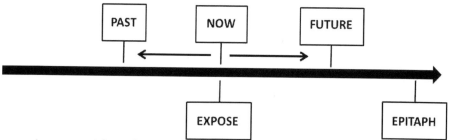

An exposé is a short write-up profiling who you are as a person. It is the disclosure of something or a public revelation. It is, inherently, about documenting the here and now.

By contrast, an epitaph is a brief writing, following death, of who an individual was. By virtue of the fact that you are alive and reading this book, this would put the epitaph at some point in your future.

So, let's start with the "exposé".

Assume you were a writer assigned to do a brief exposé on you, the person. The exposé had to be 200 words or less. Assuming total transparency, and without any "sugar coating," what would you write? Who are you?

Go ahead — do the exercise — I'll wait. It's only 200 words which is less than one typewritten page. I've provided a table for you.

PART 4 – THE EXPOSE	
QUESTION:	WHO ARE YOU?
RESPONSE: (INDICATE YOUR ANSWER IN UP TO 200 WORDS)	

It's hard isn't it?

Okay, I'll make it a bit easier.   Just write the first line of your exposé, what does that say?

It's still hard isn't it?

If done properly and honestly, this exercise can and does reveal how we see ourselves, as well as how we define ourselves, <u>today</u>!

I'm not sure about you but I know that when I have done this exercise, it's often hard for me, especially the adult me, to write the first line without using my JOB or CAREER. Why? Because in many ways that is how I see myself. That is how society has trained me to see myself and I made an agreement to accept that. So, I am a CFO and a Professor. And while I know I am a husband and father and brother, and son and, and, and — which I know intellectually are even more important roles for my life — society often places value on what we do as being synonymous with who we are.

And, unfortunately, somewhere along the line, seemingly unconsciously, I made an agreement on this.   I bought in. (Luckily, I have moved past this limited view of myself and you will too through gaining perspective.)

Take some time and finish your exposé.   Give yourself permission for it to be a rough draft. It does not need to be perfect. Just write it out.   Take no more than five to 10 minutes to capture the first thoughts you have on it. This will serve our purposes for the time being. You can always come back to it in the days and weeks ahead as you think more about it and your perspective grows.

Okay, with the exposé completed, let's move on.

For contrast, assume you were going to write your own epitaph instead. It must be 200 words or less as well. But instead of writing about who you are, write what you would like your epitaph to say.   Meaning write it based upon how you would like to be remembered. I've provided a table for you.

PART 4 – THE EPITAPH	
QUESTION:	HOW WOULD YOU LIKE TO BE REMEMBERED?
RESPONSE: *(INDICATE YOUR ANSWER IN UP TO 200 WORDS)*	

Go ahead … I'll wait (As you will find, it's easy for me to be patient as an author when all I have to do to be patient is have you set the book down long enough to complete a task… ;))

If done properly and honestly, this exercise can and does reveal how we would like to see ourselves, our "aspired" self if you will.

Alright, now for the really hard part. Compare your exposé to your epitaph.   How close are they?   What are the differences? How much daylight is there between WHO YOU ARE and WHO YOU WANT TO BE?   Why do you think there are differences? Might you have made "agreements" along the way? Might the seductive nature of the world or some fears pulled you away from who you want to be to who you are today?

Take a moment to offer your initial reflections in the table provided.

COMPARING THE EXPOSE AND THE EPITAPH

QUESTION	RESPONSE
WHAT ARE THE DIFFERENCES BETWEEN THE TWO?	
WHAT AGREEMENTS MIGHT YOU HAVE MADE THAT ARE CAUSING THE GAPS?	

J.M. Barrie, the creator of Peter Pan, once wrote:

"The Life of every man is a diary in which he means to write one story and writes another; and his humblest hour is when he compares the volume as it is with what he hoped to make it."

For me, this is a very humbling yet valuable exercise indeed! You see, in my epitaph, I desire to be someone that helped others live their lives to the fullest. I want to be remembered as someone who helped and encouraged others along that journey.

Yet, when I compare that to my exposé when I first did this exercise, there were a lot of items that were out of alignment with that epitaph. There were a lot of things I was doing and devoting time to that did not support me living my epitaph. And there were a number of agreements acting as obstacles.

For example, to live my epitaph, I want to be someone who views every person as equally important by becoming immune to the lens society might view people through — economic, religious, cultural, etc. But I have agreements I have made that I am still working through.

I want to be someone who has made themselves immune from the biases that the world might place on people and see each person as unique and important, capable of making a significant contribution to mankind. But I have agreements I have made that I am still working through.

I want to be someone who is wise and practiced in the art of trading things that are temporary — like time, money, etc — for things that are permanent — like investments in relationships, people, giving, etc. I want to be someone who has the wisdom to embody that in such a way that his life was an un-ostentatious testimony to the benefits of living that way — Peace, Contentment, Joy, Love, and Living a Full Life ! I want to live in an authentic and honest way, being the best and fullest version of myself. And while I have "agreements" on this too, the reality is, I am moving in the right direction on all fronts.

Authentic living is a journey, it is not a destination. And while my exposé is still a far cry from my desired epitaph, the gap is smaller than it was even a year ago. And closing!

14 LETTERS IN THE SAFE

I have been coping with this gap between who I am and who I want to be by writing to the important people in my life. In fact, I keep a letter in my safe to those closest to me — like my wife Melanie and my kids.

For illustration purposes, pretend that I died in a car accident on the way home tonight. Later this week, my wife Melanie is at the funeral and has the courage to stand up and say a few words about me. She would likely say I was nice, and caring, and a good provider, and a good husband, and a good father.

As my affairs are being put in order, the letter to Melanie, which I keep in the safe is brought out. She starts to read it and, paraphrasing, it says how she and the kids were always number one in my life even though I struggled to show them by the way I lived. It says how she was the inspiration for so many of the things I spent such considerable time on even though she didn't often know it. It says how I would have more aggressively and consistently courted her even after marriage if only I weren't tied up with so many other "important" (yet really "not-as-important") things.

And, given my belief in eternal life, I would be looking down on the situation as a now deceased soul, and I would ask myself one simple question — why did I need a letter in my safe to say these things when my life should have done the talking for me?

If you need a letter in your safe, you, like me, are probably not living as authentically in that portion of your life as you could.

So, let's make a commitment. Our commitment to each other is this: no more letters in the safe.

Let's replace the letters in the safe with authentic living. An authentic living where we impose who we desire to be on the world in which we live (not the other way around). Where we use our lives and trade our time to say all the things we want to say through the actions of living authentically. Through gaining perspective we can. Isn't it about time we did?

GAINING SELF PERSPECTIVE SUMMARY

"WHO ARE YOU, REALLY?"

Key Points

- You are unique and there are specific opportunities in the world perfectly suited for you.
- Knowing who you truly are and who you want to be is key to finding them.

Action Items

- Identify your dreams and aspirations.
- Identify your interests and passions.
- Identify your skills and talents.
- Write and compare your Expose and Epitaph.

PART III:

GAINING AUTHENTICITY

"Is what you do an authentic representation of who you are?"

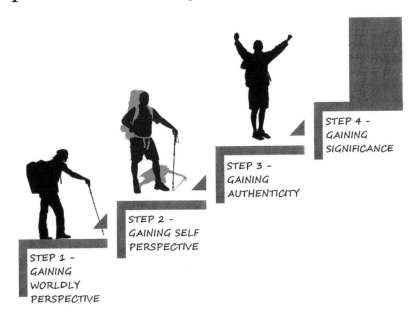

STEP 4 –
GAINING
SIGNIFICANCE

STEP 3 –
GAINING
AUTHENTICITY

STEP 2 –
GAINING SELF
PERSPECTIVE

STEP 1 –
GAINING
WORLDLY
PERSPECTIVE

In *Wisdom of the Ages*, Jim Stovall says that "wisdom is the ability to relate and apply learning to the real world." If that is true, we are going to find out how wise we really are (or are not).

If our epitaph revealed who we desire to be, our exposé represents who we are today on our journey to becoming that person. So, how do they stack up?

Perhaps as you compare who you are with who you want to be, they are in alignment and you are already living authentically with the world. If so, congratulations – you are already enjoying the spoils of authentic living.

However, if you are anything like me, your "exposé" and "epitaph" have some gaps between them. While I can articulate who I want to be in my "epitaph," it appears that who I am in the "exposé" is different. Maybe not in all areas, but certainly in some areas. So, the logical follow up questions are "Why?" and "What do I do about it?"

The reason there are gaps stems from the fact that we made agreements along the way. Agreements that came in the form of decisions to accept, consciously or unconsciously, the habits and routines that promoted that reality in our life. For example, in my life, one of my agreements was that money and materialism were important and accumulating these resources could potentially lead to the destination I was seeking. As you know, the temptation of money and materialism was heavily seductive for me.

I started to notice that more and more of my time, thoughts, and energy were going into acquiring resources which resulted from my efforts in my career. The fallout was with my wife. She got a dog to keep her company because I was at work so much. Our young marriage, while strong in many capacities, was tested unnecessarily. And the killer? My wife told me that I used to "make her feel special" and that she "didn't feel special anymore". Why? Not because of things, but because of my time. Luckily, we did not yet have kids or else they might have felt the same way.

So what did we do about it? First, I became aware of the issue and accepted responsibility for it. I owned that my intellectual desires and her importance where not being matched by where I was trading my time in life. Next, we decided to make some adjustments. We moved into a less expensive home to make finances easier and thus lessen the importance of career. Therefore, if we were going to continue to devote significant time to career, it would be by choice versus necessity — and there is a big difference. We moved toward pursuing our dreams which involved starting our family and for me specifically, becoming a college professor. And last, but not least, we started to more aggressively pursue interests and passions in our lives —which included an invitation business for her and doing more writing and speaking for me.

This was one of many agreements that the exposé and epitaph exercise helped highlight. My goal in sharing this is simply to give you a live example of how this looks.

So, with that, take a moment to really reflect on the gaps you identified between your "exposé" and your "epitaph" from the previous chapter. What are the gaps? Can you give them specific names? Write them down here:

_____

_____

_____

_____

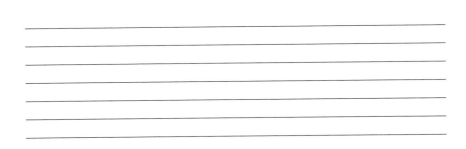

Congratulations, by simply identifying those agreements that stand in the way of becoming who you desire to be you have found the road to Authentic Living. Now, before going into detail on authentic living, let's pause for a moment and recap.

In the first two steps of gaining perspective, you gained worldly-perspective and self-perspective.

In step one you gained worldly-perspective by identifying the various roles you play in your life. Broadly, this answered the question of "What are you doing with your life now?" Furthermore, you identified fears you have as well as things you would change in the world if you could (which will be used shortly).

In step two, you gained self-perspective by focusing on answering a different question — "who are you, really?" By identifying your dreams and aspirations, interests and passions, and skills and talents, you have connected (or reconnected) with what makes you unique as an individual. Additionally, you did the heavy lifting on the exposé and epitaph to identify who you are today and who you want to be. By doing so, you have acknowledged that you are unique and there are specific opportunities in the world perfectly suited for you. Knowing who you really are and want to be is the key to finding them.

With that as your background, you will now start looking at these together and answer this question: "Is what you do an authentic representation of who you really are?"

You see, true success is living a life consistent with who you really are. It is critical to living life to the fullest. That is why step three of gaining perspective is focused on helping you answer this specific question and take action on creating authentic living in your life.

So, is what you do an authentic representation of who you really are?

If not, let me offer you the tools and encouragement you will need for the journey to authenticity.

15 AUTHENTIC LIVING AND TOOLS TO GET THERE

"To become what we are capable of becoming is the only end in life" — Robert Louis Stevenson.

<u>Tool #1: Time</u>

As we already established, time is the currency we exchange for living our lives. We trade time to experience and do life. And because it is finite, understanding where we spend our time is key to living life to the fullest.

As a result, many make the leap that we don't have enough time to live life to the fullest. But the Roman philosopher Seneca felt differently in a piece he called *On the Shortness of Life* where he contended: "It is not that we have a short time to live, but that we waste a lot of it … Life is long if you know how to use it."

Having gained perspective on who we are and want to be, we are in a position to know how to use our time wisely. And that starts with knowing where your time is currently going.

So, where do you CURRENTLY spend your time? The answer to this question will tell you what you value in your life (and it will likely confirm that you are spending most of your time on the roles you have in the world). Document where you spend your time by making a list and putting the percentage of each day (including sleeping) you spend on it. Use your "average" day or approximate as best you can. They should total 100%.

WHAT DO I CURRENTLY SPEND MY TIME ON?	
ITEM	%
GRAND TOTAL	100%

Tool #2: Prioritization

By contrast, what would you LIKE to spend your time on? This reveals what you want to be remembered for. Said a different way, it answers the question — "what will matter when you are on a rocking chair on the porch at age 90?" (ie. your epitaph).

Anthony Campolo did an interesting sociological study where he surveyed adults over 90 years old about regrets they had in life. Their responses were very telling. They stated that they would reflect more, risk more, and do more things that would live on after they are gone (legacy or significance).

With that in mind, look at your epitaph for clues on what matters most to you. What are the roles that you would like to spend time on that are in alignment with that?

WHAT I WOULD LIKE TO SPEND MY TIME ON?	
ITEM	%
GRAND TOTAL	100%

Since an example always helps, allow me to share from my own life. When I first did this exercise, one of the things I spent my time on was traveling for work. It was becoming more and more common as I was growing in this large global organization. While fun at first (partially due to seeing new places and being a young adult who did not have some of the responsibilities of family yet), it was starting to become clear that continuing down this path was going to jeopardize my ability to realize some of the things I clearly valued in my epitaph (time building my own family, being a husband and dad that was around like my parents were for me, etc). Thus, what I would LIKE to spend my time on instead of traveling on weekends to get to the Monday meeting or arriving home late from the airport exhausted and jet-lagged was BEING A PROFESSOR at a university. And while making the career change out of the global organization preceded the opportunity to become a professor by about five years, it offers an example of how clarity around what we are currently spending our time on can be changed to make space for the eventual adoption of what we would like to spend our time on.

Tool #3: Balance

Balance has always been an elusive thing for me. I have always known of its importance in a successful life. Take for example this quote from American writer Thomas Merton:

"Happiness is not a matter of intensity but of balance, order, rhythm and harmony."

I have always sought balance, but for long periods it had remained elusive as I struggled to create sustained periods of time where I felt I lived in balance.

In retrospect, a large culprit in that was not having a clear understanding of what my priorities really were. Having gained perspective and now having a better understanding of the priorities in my life, I would offer the following as my definition of balance:

"Balance is giving time to things commensurate with their true importance, not societal or worldly imposed importance."

With that said, look at where you are spending your time and compare it to where you would like to be spending your time. Are they aligned? If not, why not? What can you do about it? (I have created a simple template to assist you in working through such questions.)

AREAS NEEDING BALANCE	
QUESTIONS	RESPONSES
IS WHERE YOU SPEND YOUR TIME ALIGNED WITH WHERE YOU WOULD LIKE TO SPEND YOUR TIME?	
IF NOT, WHY NOT?	
WHAT CAN YOU DO ABOUT IT?	

Sometimes it will take a decision to change specific things (like selling a house that is too expensive or changing from a job that is not a good fit). But other times, in fact most of the time, it just takes some slight to moderate adjustments to bring about authentic living. These adjustments usually take the form of changes to our routines and habits.

Tool #4: Routines and Habits

Having identified agreements standing between who you are and who you want to be, assessed where you spend your time, prioritized where you would like to spend your time, and reconciled the two to determine the areas needing balance, you can now use the power of routines and habits to achieve that balance.

John C. Maxwell, the great leadership expert, says it this way: "You will never change your life until you change something you do daily. The secret of your success is found in your daily routine."

Aristotle's quote is not too bad either: "We are what we repeatedly do. Excellence then, is not an act, but a habit."

So here is the task. Focusing on just one "area needing balance" at a time, create a list of habits and routines that you can either add or remove from your day to better align your time and priorities.

AREA NEEDING BALANCE	
Indicate ONE AREA needing balance here: _____	
ADD or REMOVE	ROUTINE & HABIT
1. ADD or REMOVE	
2. ADD or REMOVE	
3. ADD or REMOVE	
4. ADD or REMOVE	
5. ADD or REMOVE	

Allow me to give an example to illustrate how routines and habits can be used to promote balance.

As I have shared previously, money and materialism are seductive parts of the world for me. Having received an education in and made a career out of finance and accounting, I have strengthened skills that have led me to constantly assess value based upon numbers on a sheet. This manifested itself in my own life in a number of destructive ways.

I used to go onto E*Trade and the equivalent market websites to check my investment and retirement accounts on a daily basis. This routine or habit created a perpetual spotlight on measuring my success by a number on a screen which equated to my net worth. Knowing that I had a predisposition to be seduced by the money and materialism in the world and the fear of not having enough, this was adding to that addiction and problem, not reducing it.

So, after identifying this as an agreement I had made and a gap between who I was and who I wanted to be, I changed my routines and habits to promote balance.

Rather than reviewing these items daily, I decided to take a more practical approach. I started doing a quarterly review. It was often enough that I felt I could adequately review the progress of personal investments and take corrective measures when necessary. But it was not so often that I found my self-worth in the values produced by the market close each day.

While difficult at first, over time, it slowly lowered the importance of money and materialism in my life. By removing the daily lookup of my financial position (a routine I STOPPED), it created time in my schedule to ADD in routines that would promote more balance — like being fully present to talk to my wife at dinner instead (something I wanted to spend my time on). While seemingly simple, it had what Darren Hardy calls "The Compound Effect" in his book by the same name. Making meaningful change in your life is the result of making small changes in your daily habits and routines. In my case, it meant removing one habit that was causing imbalance and adopting another habit that was needed to bring about more balance. (By the way, if you are interested in a deeper dive on how habits and routines — along with other valuable tools — play a large role in determining our success, I highly recommend checking out Darren's book. In particular, his recommendations on creating habits and routines at the beginning and end of your day are fantastic.)

Now, as with everything, there are pros and cons to using routines and habits to achieve balance. The pros, some of which I have already alluded to, are that habits and routines properly implemented can indeed be effective in raising or reducing the importance of various items in our lives. It is said that to create a new habit it takes a minimum of 21 days to develop (though recent research may suggest it may take more like a few months). Translation — it will take a commitment.

But there are cons to. Creating a bunch of routines and habits can seem rote or contrived — especially early on in the process. Remember, our sole purpose is to be authentic. These are just tools to get there. Guard against creating routines and habits of trying to be something you actually are not. Be sure this is really a priority and authentically you.

Also, creating too many adjustments to routines and habits at one time can start to feel like a "to-do list." Remember, habits and routines are a tool to try to help raise or lessen the importance of items that are incorrectly prioritized. Over time, they become natural to you (especially if they are authentic to you). You don't want things, especially things like reading stories to your kids or talking with family members on the phone for example, to feel like chores on the "to-do list." Thus, you may want to consider using the habits and routines on only a few key items at a time, so it's manageable and not overwhelming. Once those become an automatic part of your life, then move on to a few others.

As we close on the use of habits and routines to promote balance, allow me to share *"The Story of the Cherokee and the Wolf"* to drive this point home:

An old Cherokee told his grandson, "My son there is a battle between two wolves inside us all. One is Evil. It is Anger, Resentment, Jealousy, Greed, Inferiority, Lies and Ego. The other is Good. It is Joy, Peace, Love, Hope, Humanity, Kindness, Empathy, and Truth."

The boy thought about it and asks, "Grandfather, which wolf wins?"

The old man quietly replied, "The one you feed."

In many ways, the habits and routines help us feed our wolf. Make sure you are feeding the one you want to win.

16 LESSONS FOR AUTHENTIC LIVING

The fact that there are so many options available in the world for us to pursue is exciting. But it can also add complication and be overwhelming. Frankly, the sheer number of things we can spend our time on can act as forks in the road to throw us off course. They have a way of mystifying, confusing, or seducing us into paths that may not be right for us. They take on different forms but the result is usually the same — they can create greater gaps between WHO WE ARE (Exposé) and WHO WE WANT TO BE (Epitaph).

So how do we stay the course? Having gained worldly perspective and self-perspective, we have answered some of the key questions we need to pursue authentic living. And while it is true that we have our habits and routines to keep our balance, are there any other things we should know for the journey?

The answer, of course, is yes. And they have to do with the concept of moving from question to exclamation in life.

Gaining worldly perspective and gaining self-perspective were both about answering questions. By taking the time and doing the work to answer the questions, the context was available to start to pursue authentic living.

But the ability to grow in your authentic living comes down to being able to continue to answer questions and think critically for your life.   With that ability, comes the answers from which you can clearly make decisions and live with exclamation in your life.

In other words, if I were to draw a picture, the ability for you to live authentically (with exclamation) has its foundation on the answers you received from asking questions. The more questions you gain clarity on, the more perspective you have to live authentically.

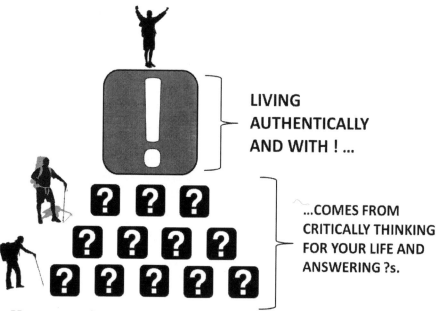

LIVING
AUTHENTICALLY
AND WITH ! ...

...COMES FROM
CRITICALLY THINKING
FOR YOUR LIFE AND
ANSWERING ?s.

Here are a few lessons that I have learned or been taught by mentors that should help in perpetuating authenticity and retaining perspective. By gaining your answer to the posed question, you will be able to live your life with more authenticity and exclamation.

Lesson #1 — Which are the Right Opportunities in Life to Pursue?

One key component of living an authentic life revolves around choosing the right paths. This can be hard at times, as the roads intertwine and the map is unclear. The best tool I have found for assessing the paths goes something like this:

Imagine a bunch of converging arrows. Put Skills and Talents in one, Interests and Passions in another, and Dreams and Aspirations in a third. Authentic living can be found in opportunities in life which allow you to find common ground for all three.

More simply stated, the right opportunities to pursue living life to the fullest will usually be in alignment with your dreams and aspirations, allow you to pursue your interests and passions, and make use of your skills and talents.

I often find myself drawing this picture when talking to my students. As mentioned, they regularly come into my office and ask my opinion on what career path they should consider. Rather than answering their question directly, I take them through questions relating to their own skills and talents, interests and passions, and dreams and aspirations so they can gain perspective on the answer for themselves.

One example that stands out was an undergraduate student from a few years ago. He had great skills and talents in finance and numbers in general. And he knew he wanted to use them in something he believed in, but didn't know how to find it.

So I started talking him through the spectrum of the finance industry. For example, the differences between investment finance, financial advising, and corporate finance. We talked through the nature of careers in all of those paths including likely financial gains and time commitments.

Having identified that the corporate finance role seemed most authentic to who he was, we proceeded to look at what he was interested in and passionate about. I asked him questions like "what is it that when you do it, you lose track of time?" or "if you had some unexpected free time, what would you like to do?". His answers included that he liked being active and outdoors (hiking, etc) and liked cars.

Okay, I then asked him whether he envisioned himself working for a large, medium, or small sized organization — taking him through the differences of each. How large organizations may be able to offer specialization and a focused training program. In contrast, how small organizations would likely have him learning multiple departments and functions where he would jump from one to the next to the next throughout the day. And so forth.

Having determined that starting with a large organization was authentic to him, we then focused on his dreams and aspirations. Ten to twenty years from now, what did he desire his career to look like? Where did it fit relative to the rest of his desires for his life? While hard at first, he was able to describe his vision well enough to gain a reasonably clear answer.

By gaining perspective on his dreams and aspirations, skills and talents, and interests and passions, finding opportunities that were congruent or authentic became the easier part. We identified large corporations, in the lifestyle or automobile industries, that had internship opportunities that could lead to corporate finance roles.

And in so doing, this student was able to trade their time during one college summer to gain valuable life experience on whether this truly was an authentic career path for them.

But irrespective of whether it was a potential career being considered, or a decision on some other aspect of life, authenticity is the result of finding opportunities in alignment with your dreams and aspirations, allowing you to pursue your interests and passions, while simultaneously making use of your skills and talents. Such opportunities lead to living life to the fullest. And it provides a simple and easy way to test out a path for authenticity.

Are there opportunities for authenticity in your life that you have not acted on? What is inauthentic in your life that you need to stop? Take a moment and place your answers below.

_____

_____

_____

_____

_____

_____

_____

_____

_____

_____

_____

_____

_____

_____

_____

_____

_____

_____

_____

_____

_____

_____

Utilize the diagram if it helps as it prompts some of the questions we have covered relating to Dreams and Aspirations, Interests and Passions, and Skills and Talents.

1 What did you dream about doing with your life growing up? What did you want to be?

2 What is it, that when you do it, time seems to fly by? When you have free time, you love to _____?

3 What are you comparatively better at than others? Where do you get to put these skills and talents to use in your life?

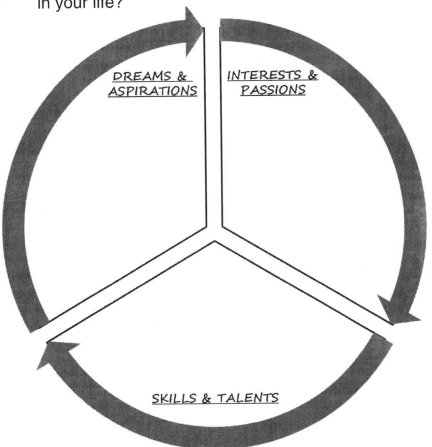

DREAMS & ASPIRATIONS

INTERESTS & PASSIONS

SKILLS & TALENTS

Lesson #2 — Do you know how to say "no?"

Part of knowing what path to take in life also means you must say "no" to other paths. At times this can be very hard, especially when both paths are of interest.

As we have covered, there are a lot of invitations in life that will ask you to commit your time. Unfortunately, many of these invitations will be inconsistent with the journey to living your life to the fullest. At times, they will come from friends, associates, and family who will be hard to say "no" to. But you need to learn to be able to say "no" when the invitation extended to you is inconsistent with your path.

Sometimes, you will need to say "no" because you need some time to yourself. Sometimes you will need to say "no" because it is at odds with your values. Other times you will need to say "no" because you just don't want to.

I am not saying don't make compromises or sacrifices and only do what you want. But keeping the doors of opportunity perpetually propped open can be exhausting.

The solution is knowing how to say no by being able to have clarity on when to say "yes". This is one of the gifts of gaining perspective.

Where do you need to say "no" in your life? What are the things you are currently doing that you need to say "no" to in the future? Can you opt out now? Why or why not?

_____

_____

_____

_____

Lesson #3 — How Much is Enough?

As mentioned previously, many people, myself included, find it difficult to answer the question of "How Much is Enough?" It is a question I often get from my students as well. "Professor Munson, how do I know how much is enough _____ (studying, money, etc)?"

We have learned experientially, often through school, that if we simply put in more effort, we get rewarded with the outcome we want. For example, if we study harder, we get an A. If we practice more, we will perform better on our sports team.

While this creates a good work ethic, it also creates an implied, but false, conclusion — that by putting in more effort, we can achieve the outcome we desire. And thus, we start to think we can achieve success by putting in more. In other words, we start to think we can control outcomes by the effort we put in.

What that agreement does not tell you is the cost you pay for doing such.

I will never forget the story a friend told me about a senior executive at a Fortune 100 technology company he knew. The executive's schedule was so demanding that if his wife or kids wanted to see him or get help with their homework, they had to call his secretary to schedule a time to meet with him. This stuck out to me because it begs the question of "how much is enough?"

There did not seem to be any boundaries. Work took precedence over everything. The answer to "how much is enough?" was "whatever it takes that we can fit into 24 hours!" And while I did not know this man or his family, it left me wondering what the long term implications for him and his family would be as a result of their current answer to "how much is enough?"

So how do we know when enough is enough? It has to come from perspective and wisdom. Perspective in knowing that doing your best is all you can do given all the things that you are spending time on that are important. Wisdom in being able to define what doing your best is while not mortgaging those other aspects of your life. Finding that line will be different for everyone. But everyone must find that line or else the default answer becomes "whatever it takes".

Where are you needing to gain more clarity on how much is enough in your life? Do you know how much is enough there? Can you draw the line in the sand? What is that line? Who do you need to tell?

_____

_____

_____

_____

_____

_____

_____

_____

_____

_____

_____

_____

_____

_____

_____

Lesson #4 — Focus on what you can control ... then let go of the outcome.

Mark Twain once said, "I've lived through some terrible things in my life, some of which actually happened."

I think his point may be that we worry about things we don't need to.

While I don't have the magic pill for worrying, I do know that I have spent a disproportionate amount of my life worrying about many things, most of which I cannot control. Thus, logic tells us, we may be able to eliminate those.

There is a great quote by an unknown author that says "Today is the tomorrow that you worried about yesterday"

Think about that.

Now, how many TODAYS could you have enjoyed by not worrying about them when they were not yet upon you and out of your control to begin with?

My answer is A LOT!

Moreover, what if you just focused on what you could control and let go of the rest? By focusing on what you can control as a replacement for what you cannot control, you are able to still occupy your mind but with something of logical value. Then, while you can use what you can control to try to achieve the desired outcome, you inject perspective to let go of that outcome. Especially if it resulted from the things you could not control.

These are simple ingredients for success and authenticity in life.

What have you been trying to control that you need to let go of? What are the things you can control that you can focus on instead?

116

(Remember to keep them in check with knowing "how much is enough" from Lesson #3)

_____

_____

_____

_____

_____

_____

_____

_____

_____

_____

_____

_____

_____

_____

_____

_____

_____

_____

Lesson #5 — How to use affirmations to stay encouraged on the journey.

It is hard to be authentic. Often times, living authentically means that you are cutting against the well-developed societal paths of the world. In such circumstances, you are going to run into resistance and friction.

It may come in the form of negativity or judgment being cast your way by others. This is likely due to the fact that you are being perceived as doing something different or strange. Some simply won't understand it.

It may also come in the form of friction due to the fact that the path you are charting is not well-traveled. Because it has not been as often traveled, it is exhausting to gain ground on such (think of the difference between driving on a paved road versus driving where no road exists).

For many who are trying to live authentically, one of the biggest obstacles can be that feeling of discouragement that comes from both the negativity of others or exhaustion of pursuing less-traveled paths. So here is a solution to help you get through those times. And it may sound a bit egotistical, but it's not. It's effective. And being effective on being authentic is not egotistical — it's being you.

Consider keeping a box or folder of the letters and affirmations that you have received in life. They may come in the form of a letter from a friend, an email from some co-workers, a birthday or holiday card with a nice message, or other similar communication. Often times, people encourage us or appreciate us but we quickly forget. If you printed it out, three hole punched it, and put it into a binder, you might be surprised how quickly the binder fills up.

For me, the binder includes letters from students, employees, bosses, family members, and friends that have encouraged me. Some might call this type of binder a "brag book" that is narcissistic in nature. I don't think so. I don't have it sitting out for every guest who comes in my home to view it. In fact, it is in a closet completely out of sight where only I know where to find it.

It serves as a valuable tool to have the courage to live authentically. Every once in a while, when I am feeling down or ready to throw in the towel, I will pull it out and it will remind me that what I am doing is important and matters to others around me. So often we forget about these people in our corner which is why having a visual that you can reach for when needed, can help tremendously.

Do you have affirmations that you can use as encouragement? Who are they from and what did they say? Where are they and can you pull them together for ease of reference from time to time?

_____

_____

_____

_____

_____

_____

_____

_____

_____

_____

_____

_____

Lesson #6 — Do you stop to ask "why"?

If you want to live an authentic life, you must stop to think during your life. I know it sounds trite but we often skip right past crucial points in our lives without recognizing we just missed a question, did not give an answer, and thus, implicitly made an agreement. Instead we accept the "societal pathway" and keep moving.

The fix is to develop critical thinking skills. In fact, in many ways, if my students only walk with the ability to think critically about things — turning questions into exclamations — that is still an extremely favorable outcome (even if they forget the details of the discounted cash flow model I taught them in my valuations class).

Why, you might ask? Good question.

The Critical Thinking Community frames the problem this way:

"Everyone thinks. It is our nature to do so. But much of our thinking, left to itself, is biased, distorted, partial, uninformed, or downright prejudiced. Yet, the quality of our life and that of what we produce, make, or build depends precisely on the quality of our thought. Shoddy thinking is costly, both in money and in quality of life. Excellence in thought, however, must be systematically cultivated."

In case assignments that my students must complete, a significant portion of their grade comes from them articulating why they came to the answer or conclusion they did. Irrespective of whether I agree with the conclusion or not, I am extremely interested in whether they can support their conclusion clearly.

So, while there are formal studies and models around this, I adopt a simple and practical approach. In order to think critically for our lives, simply stop and ask the question "why?" And ask it approximately three to five times (as we illustrated previously). This is critical thinking in its purest form.

This will force you to get to the root of the things that you do in your life. If they are inauthentic, this line of questioning will reveal it.

Here is a silly example to illustrate my point:

#1 Why do I need a car when I turn 16?

Potential Answer: To get around.

#2 Why do I need to get around?

Potential Answer: To go to school and work.

#3 Why do I need to go to school and work?

Potential Answer: To learn and earn money.

#4 Why do I need to be the one to drive myself to school and work?

Potential Answer: I don't since my parents can take me or I can take the bus.

#5 Therefore, why do I really need a car?

Potential Answer: I don't. I really just want one because it's cool and can give me freedom.

It is noteworthy that asking yourself what the alternative could be and the pros and cons of the alternative may also reveal valuable information, especially on big decisions.

Ultimately, we may end up choosing the "societal pathway" as a result of our conclusion. But at least it will be a conscious selection and authentic to who we are instead of an unconscious agreement.

What do you need to stop and ask "5 whys" about in your own life?

_____

_____

_____

_____

_____

_____

_____

_____

_____

_____

_____

_____

_____

_____

_____

_____

_____

_____

Lesson #7 — Does our upbringing or family of origin define us?

Part of living authentically means we inherently believe we have the choice and ability to change our circumstance. That no matter our upbringing or family of origin, we have the ability to gain perspective and make decisions for ourselves based upon that perspective.

For example, if you are brought up to hate a race of people or a country, that may be the way you feel because it has been your reality for as long as you can remember. (In other words, it may just be a routine or habit that has been practiced for many years.)

However, you might ask yourself, have you ever actually met anyone from that race or country that you dislike? Why do you dislike them? Have you met people from your own country or race that you dislike? Why do you dislike them? Are the reasons similar? What does that mean?

Many of our views in life are shaped by others and these are often the earliest and most deeply rooted agreements we accept (and many we are not even conscious of in many cases). The reason they are often so strong is that they are beliefs that have existed the longest and thus, we have had the most practice in reaffirming them.

Do you have any deep rooted beliefs that you should take a look at? If so, list them here.

_____

_____

_____

Be sure you have thoroughly asked and questioned why you believe a certain way and whether you truly believe it is justified. This is crucially important to your authenticity.

17 THEN WHAT?

Have you ever bought a lottery ticket? A ticket that could win a jackpot of say $100 million? Taking a mathematician's view, the chance of you winning the lottery on the popular "Powerball" game is in the range of 1 in 175 million. Yet, if you are like me, you may have dreamed about what you would do if, by some slight chance, you were the winner.

So, let's try it out. The jackpot is $100 million. Let's say you will have $50 million after taxes.

What would you do with it?

Buy a new car? A new house? Get some things for your friends? Eat at some fancy restaurants? Stay in the suite of a five-star hotel and order room service?

I know my answer. I would probably start by investing it — boring I know — buying things that would provide me a return on that money (likely residential real estate I could rent out). I would also probably blow some of it on fun things as well and perhaps a newer car though I love my Expedition with over 200,000 miles on it.

OK, so, let's say we do whatever it is what we would do with it. Then what?

Well, again, for some, the money equals freedom to not have to work — assuming they would choose that route. In my case, I am not sure that I would since working, when in balance, is authentically me. But, assuming the money gave us more of that finite resource called time back, then I would use more of that time to spend with the family, travel, go see the world, do some more hikes, and so on.

OK, so, let's say we do whatever it is we would do with that additional time. Then what?

There are only so many places I can go. So many things I can see. Sooner or later, especially if money was no object, I would experience what economists call the law of diminishing utility, meaning I do not get the same level of happiness out of the money and free time that I once did.

OK, so, the "then what" phenomenon reveals a problem doesn't it?

Once you continue to ask "then what" enough times, you will find that there are no more answers you can give that will make you feel successful and realize the happiness you originally experienced. Some say this represents the end of the "honeymoon stage of sudden wealth" where the excitement of winning the lottery and the resources it provides get replaced with the reality that money cannot buy happiness.

Bottom line: something is still missing. Something that cannot be filled with more consumption.

But perhaps winning the lottery is an easy example. So let's flip to a more devastating one. What if you were in a tragic car accident and paralyzed? Then what?

For my part, I would be very, very angry. And very depressed. Asking questions like why did this happen to me?

Then what?

I might be unable to do my job or severely limited in my ability to do it.

Then what?

I may be unable to provide for my family which could create financial pressures and potentially marriage and family challenges and stress.

Then what?

And this could go on and on through various stages of coping with this terrible tragedy until, somewhere down the line, there was acceptance.

Then what?

Then, after accepting it, I would ultimately come back to the same conclusion as with the lottery ticket example. I would start to desire something bigger with my life again. That whether we have money or are facing a tragedy, the reality is we are looking still, even in completely different circumstances, for something bigger in life.

The success brought about by living authentically can lead to great rewards. It is about getting. And as a result it can lead to happiness.

But because it's about getting, the happiness is temporary. What we are looking for is something that cannot be taken away. Something that cannot disappear. Something even bigger. Something that has a more perpetual meaning.

What we are looking for is significance.

GAINING AUTHENTICTY SUMMARY

"IS WHAT YOU DO AN AUTHENTIC REPRESENTATION OF WHO YOU ARE?"

Key Points

- Authentic living is true success.
- Success can lead to great rewards – mainly happiness.
- But because success is about getting, the happiness is temporary.

Action Items

- Identify where you are spending your time currently.
- Identify where you would like to be spending your time.
- Identify the gaps that need to be addressed.
- Establish the habits and routines necessary to get there.

PART IV:

GAINING SIGNIFICANCE

"Will what you do last beyond you?"

STEP 4 –
GAINING
SIGNIFICANCE

STEP 3 –
GAINING
AUTHENTICITY

STEP 2 –
GAINING SELF
PERSPECTIVE

STEP 1 –
GAINING
WORLDLY
PERSPECTIVE

On April 14, 1912, at approximately 11:40 PM, an unsinkable ship hit an iceberg. Some two hours later, the Titanic had sunk below the ocean's surface on her journey to the bottom of the North Atlantic.

By all accounts, there were a number of successful people on that ship including American millionaire John Jacob Astor IV, industrialist Benjamin Guggenheim, Macy's owner Isidor Straus, and numerous others. These were people who had accomplished or achieved much in their life, the byproducts of which included great financial resources at their disposal, power through companies they owned, and prestige through the upper class society to which they belonged. These were all the things they had gained as a result of their success.

Yet what was the constant that everyone, irrespective of their class of ticket, faced that night in April of 1912? The answer, of course, is that all of their success would be taken away as that unsinkable ship sank.

Then what is the point? If everything we have gained in life, all of the fruits of our work can be taken away and is out of our control, what is the point?

I will always remember a sermon I heard when I was a very young adult. Having used the Titanic and its unsinkable image as a backdrop, the pastor asked us to reflect on the lives we were living. Then, in a solemn moment, he asked us to answer just one simple question — if we were on that ship on the morning of April 14, 1912, would we spend our day rearranging the deck chairs?

Of course, any effort we put toward rearranging deck chairs would go down with the ship. So, if we only had a day left, would we use that time on something that would die with us?

The truth is that success is very much about what we gain or achieve. A promotion at work. A personal best in the 5k run we have been training for. The new and bigger home or car. A good investment which increases our bank account. And while these can lead to happiness, it does not lead to sustained and long-term peace and contentment because it is fundamentally about getting. And the act of getting is a temporary one.

Furthermore, there is something even more troubling about success. Even assuming we obtained success — if it is about getting — then the reality is that it could all be taken away, just like it was for all of those "successful" people aboard that Titanic.

For example, if my success is found in my home, it could be taken away by natural disaster, foreclosure, and numerous other ways. If my success is found in a position I occupy, that could be taken away as I could be fired or replaced or the company could go away. If my success is found in my bank accounts and retirement accounts that give me peace of mind, they could be taken away by a market crash, inflation, or a number of other circumstances. If my success is found in the perception people have of me due to a beautiful wife and family, that could be taken away by my wife leaving me, or in a tragedy, or a number of other ways. If my success is found in my health and ability to do things physically, my health could be taken away as I could get sick, or just get older and slowly my body gets tired.

My point is that success is temporary. And while this is depressing to think about, which is not my intention, the point is that all of this is actually out of our control.

This was a great revelation for me, especially as a "finance guy" because I had been trained to evaluate things from a numbers and resources perspective. It was about assessing risk *vs.* reward, probability, and the likelihood of an outcome. All of them have risk. So I found myself constantly trying to protect my returns while minimizing risk. But no matter how far I went on any of it, I could not take out all of the risk.

And the reason? Because, in this world, everything can be taken away. It's not all within our control. And to think otherwise, would be to continue to rearrange deck chairs on a sinking ship.

Or, as country singer George Strait put it in his song "You'll Be There" — "You don't bring nothing with you here and you don't bring nothing back. I've never seen a hearse, with a luggage rack".

As I reflected on my own life, I feel blessed to have achieved a number of successes early on in my life. And despite being out of balance some between who I am and who I want to be, I would say that on the whole, I have experienced my fair share of success for which I am very grateful.

However, even with all of that, something was missing. Something that was bigger than me. If simply achieving success could lead to sustained and long-term peace and contentment, I would have found it — trust me, I had looked.

The result of this realization was that I never quite felt content in any success I experienced. And it never lasted. I continued to work harder and harder to try to protect against the temporary nature of it. To keep the accolades and achievements coming in. To keep the money and resources coming my way. And this may be partly why I got out of balance on the career element due to wanting "more resources" to protect against the prospects of losing the ones I had. I did not know what to do other than work harder and dive deeper into the world. All those years, if I wanted to perform better on a test, I studied more and harder. If I wanted to be a better basketball player, I practiced more. As I have shared, the correlation became drilled into my head that harder work equals better outcome. Or, said differently, I thought I had the ability to control the outcome through hard work.

While this was the knee-jerk reaction, it was wrong. At best, I could influence the outcome ... *maybe*.

18 THE SIGNIFICANCE OF GIVING

Feeling disenchanted by the temporary nature of success, I asked myself the question of whether anything exists that cannot be taken away?

That journey led me to a significant find and it came in the form of giving.

Whereas success was all about gaining, significance was all about giving since it focuses on other people. Significance actually gives purpose to success.

When you give, you don't have to worry about things being out of your control. You don't have to worry about protecting things from being taken away. Why? Because the nature of giving is that you don't actually hold on to or own anything.

And in case there was any doubt, here were some quotes that really drove this point home:

"What we have done for ourselves alone dies with us. What we have done for others and the world remains and is immortal."
— Albert Pike, American attorney, soldier, writer

"We make a living by what we get, but we make a life by what we give."
— Winston Churchill

"You aren't wealthy until you have something money can't buy."
— Garth Brooks

"Only a life lived for others is a life worthwhile."
— Albert Einstein

While consumption-based success is temporary, significance gives us the ability to achieve meaning through giving. And all the things we desired to get from success — joy, peace, contentment — are actually available in perpetuity through the meaning that follows significance. This was a key breakthrough in gaining perspective.

19 NO MATTER WHAT SIZE, IT IS ALWAYS SIGNIFICANT

Perhaps the best way to illustrate that power of significance is with this story. I recently had the opportunity to hear the journey of a man named Bob, who is deceased, as presented by his daughter.

The year was 1947 and Bob was a youth evangelist for a non-profit organization whose purpose was to share their faith in China. He thought it was going to be a one-time summer mission trip — an opportunity where he would apply his interest and passion for his faith by using his skills and talents of teaching and speaking.

On one of the last days of the trip, he met a missionary teacher named Tena. She presented him a beaten and abandoned 11-year-old girl named White Jade who, in response to Bob's testimony, had given her life to the faith and was subsequently beaten by her family.

Unable to care for the child, Tena brought this issue to Bob and shared her story. Bob had no idea how to respond to this circumstance, after all, this was the last day of what Bob viewed as a one-time summer mission trip. Bob asked Tena what she was going to do. Tena turned the question on Bob and said, "The question is not what am I going to do about it. The question, Bob Pierce, is what are you going to do about it?"

In our lives, our opportunities for significance will come in the form of what we can do for others. The right opportunities will be the ones that are in alignment with who we authentically are — the intersection of our dreams and aspirations, interests and passions, and skills and talents. And sometimes, like with Bob, they may come at inconvenient or unanticipated times.

So what did Bob do? Bob gave the woman his last five dollars (a lot of money in 1947) and agreed to send the same amount each month to help the woman care for this girl. And in that moment, it is believed that the seed for what would become the global organization World Vision, was born.

Bob made a decision that day, partially the result of courage and partially the result of perspective — to live significantly by weaving the needs of others into his life — and in so doing, created the foundation of what is now a $1 billion global organization with a vision of every child having life to the fullest. An organization that offers 4.3 million children support worldwide. An organization that serves in 1,650 communities globally. An organization that intervened in response to 89 major disaster and emergency responses. And all this just in the year 2014.

Now that's significance.

And it's worth noting, all it took was Bob taking one step by seeing an opportunity and filling it. In that act, the first ripple gave rise to the opportunity for others to find their significance too. It is through that consistent pursuit of significance by so many that this particular organization has achieved what it has. And so goes the story of many other causes, movements, and acts of significance. One person (Bob) filling an opportunity for their own significance charts a path for others to be presented with opportunities for significance in the future.

Which reminds me of a well-known story — credited to Loren Eiseley, an American anthropologist — which gets at the heart of the issue.

A boy is throwing starfish back into the ocean, one at a time, as the tide is rolling out and the sun is getting hotter. The sand is littered with thousands of starfish which will die if not thrown back — making this a monumental task that the boy is not likely to make a significant difference on — a fact a nearby observer makes to the boy.

The boy, acknowledging the comment, picks up another starfish and, throwing it back, says, "I made a difference to that one."

It's not the ultimate scale of the impact that matters. Had Bob only made a difference to the one girl, it still would have been significant. Bob answered the opportunity to give something that could not be taken away. And in so doing, his significance cannot be taken away.

What beach are you walking? Are there any starfish in your path that you can throw back?

20 THE PARADOX OF
SIGNIFICANCE – IT'S A WIN-WIN

Life didn't make sense until significance was part of my perspective. It finally offered something that cannot be taken away. Something that mattered beyond me. I found a great personal example of significance during a mission trip I made to the small villages of Umzimvubu, South Africa in 2012. Here is an excerpt from my reflections on that trip:

Life is a funny thing. On the one hand, the people in this region have needs that most of us take for granted. I don't give it a second thought when I turn on the water in my home or go to the fridge to get a snack. Going to school and having trained teachers and proper resources was a foregone conclusion. And having a roof over my head was something that everyone I know seemed to have. So the thought of someone not having it was foreign.

You would think that with these basic needs being met, the quality of my life would far supersede those of the people we met in Umzimvubu. That by not having to worry about where my next meal is coming from, that I would somehow have more happiness, peace, and joy.

But, if I am being honest, having spent the week in Umzimvubu, I would be kidding myself if I said that I was richer in life than these people. If we measure success based on things that money can't buy, these people, and especially the children, have it. Never have I seen a more joyous and happy people who seemed to have nothing to be joyous and happy about.

And thus, the paradox is this — that we (with many resources) are in a position to help these people with meeting their basic needs to survive — and they (with the simplicity and clarity of perspective) are in a position to reciprocate with helping us to realize some key truths that can enrich our lives — both, ultimately leading to living life to the fullest for the other.

21 A LIFE OF SIGNIFICANCE

Do you desire more than just success in your life? Do you desire something that cannot be taken away? Something that is bigger than you? Do you desire to weave it into your day to day life? A significance so profound that it will even outlast your own life?

The best way to find significance is to look for opportunities where your dreams and aspirations, interests and passions, and skills and talents collide with the needs of others. In fact, the only difference between authenticity and significance is that significance is not only authentic but also includes the needs of others in the framework.

Aristotle said it this way, *"Where your talents and the needs of the world cross — there lies your vocation."*

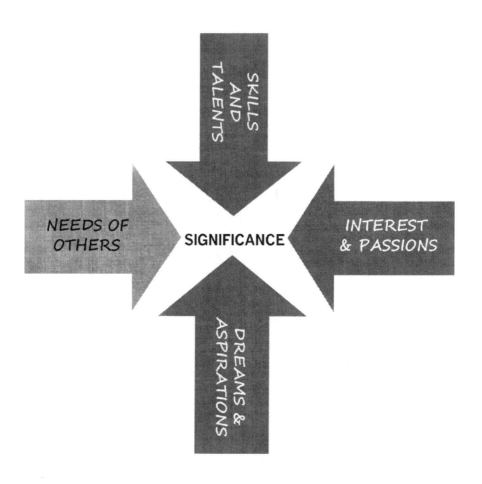

You may have some opportunities for significance right in front of you that you don't recognize as such. By the same token, you may have some opportunities that you can see but just need to act on. Using this framework as a guide, make a list of the following:

A. All of the things in your life that cannot be taken away!

THINGS THAT CANNOT BE TAKEN AWAY	
1.	
2.	
3.	

This is not a trick question. I put only three spots as it is hard to find things that cannot be taken away. Give it some thought and then populate it as best you can.

B. Where might there be opportunities for you to find significance by including the needs of others in your daily life?

OPPORTUNITIES FOR SIGNIFICANCE	
1.	
2.	
3.	
4.	
5.	

It has been my experience that we sometimes have to start our search for significance by intentionally finding opportunities to serve the needs of others in opportunities where our Dreams and Aspirations, Skills and Talents, and Interest and Passions collide with those Needs. For example, I recall having a number of coaches over the years who had dreams and aspirations of playing pro sports when they were young, had great skills and talents in the sport, and had an interest and passion for the sport — let's say basketball. They combined those with the needs of others — young basketball players like me — through coaching youth teams or conducting summer basketball camps. While a simple example, as a young and aspiring basketball player myself, I looked to those who were further along the journey to give me guidance and coaching to help me realize my highest potential as a player. This, in and of itself, gave those coaches a platform to have significance in my life. Luckily for me, I had many great coaches who not only taught me basketball, but helped me learn valuable life lessons that shaped who I am today. As a result, I feel grateful to those platforms and people and desire to try to give back in much the same way.

That said, the amazing thing about significance is that it seems to pick up momentum. It seems that over time, through the slight adjustments that daily habits and routines provided, coupled with keeping our eyes out for the right opportunities to include the needs of others in our lives, we start to find that virtually everything we do can be significant.

For example, when I was first coming to the conclusion that significance was the end I was looking for in life, I started to explore different opportunities proactively to test it out. One of those was helping with a church high school group. While I only did it for a couple of years, and it wasn't the perfect fit for me for a number of reasons, it did provide me the opportunity to share life lessons with these students. Their response and desire for more information on these types of topics revealed that I had an interest and passion in sharing such information, and that I was reasonably skilled and talented at delivering the message. It also exposed that I have a dream and aspiration to have an impact on improving the lives of others through teaching and sharing.

Knowing this about myself now, I kept my eyes peeled for opportunities in life to meet these needs of others in the things I did in my everyday life. The result has been an exciting combination of increased authenticity and simultaneous infusion of significance.

When the opportunity to teach at the university presented itself, it was now much more than just being a teacher on the subjects of accounting and finance. It was a place where I could achieve my dreams and aspirations of being a professor, use my interests and passions in sharing and teaching, and my skills and talents in speaking and delivering content, to meet the needs of students in the growth of their subject knowledge but also their ability to do critical thinking in preparation for life.

Because I had been able to give significance a name and place in my perspective, I was able to see things with much more meaning. And the result is viewing that role as far more than just a "job". In other words, significance wasn't something I did as one component of my life. Rather, by taking this approach, I was de-compartmentalizing my life and opening it up to find significance woven into all parts.

The same goes for my role as CFO which I had been even prior to this revelation. Putting that through the same test, I now saw an opportunity to:

- Fulfill my dreams and aspirations of being part of a team and helping them achieve their goals

- In an area of interest and passion which is the real estate industry where we build homes for people to raise their families and build community

- Using my skills and talents in accounting and finance and leadership

- To meet the needs of:

    o Our employees — to have a great place to come work where they could learn, be supported, and become their highest and best version of themselves

149

o Our customers — to have a company that makes their real estate experience, which is one of the most stressful events of our lives, less so due to the efficiency, communication, and organization with which we service them

o Our owners — to support them realizing their vision for the business and supporting their ability to provide for their families and the families of those whose paychecks they sign (including my own)

And frankly, I could go on and on. That is what is so exciting about gaining perspective through the fourth step of significance. Over time, it becomes a natural part of your life – the common thread for everything you spend your time on.

Simply stated, here are the points I want you to walk away with:

- Success, while it provides happiness, is temporary, because it's based upon what we get.

- Significance is perpetual because it's based upon what we give — and what we give cannot be taken away. It gives meaning to our lives which allows us to enjoy the more perpetual feelings of joy, contentment and peace that we really seek.

- Significance comes from including the needs of others in the framework of our lives.

- The best opportunities for finding significance will be where your Dreams and Aspirations, Interests and Passions, and Skills and Talents collide with the Needs of Others.

Significance is the end so many of us are actually seeking when we set out on the road to be "successful". What we are hoping we will find with success are sustained periods of peace, joy, contentment, and meaning. Yet only through finding significance in your life, by including the needs of others in your framework, will you find what you are looking for.

So I leave you with this one question to ponder — will what you are doing last beyond you? If so, congratulations, you are living significantly.

GAINING SIGNIFICANCE SUMMARY
"WILL WHAT YOU DO LAST BEYOND YOU?"

Key Points

- Including the needs of others is the key to living with significance.
- It provides meaning, which results in more permanent joy, peace, and contentment because its based upon what you give, not what you get.

Action Items

- Identify the opportunities for significance in your life – the places where your skills and talents, interests and passions, and dreams and aspirations collide with the needs of others.

CONCLUSION

"Living Your Life to the Fullest"

22 AUTHENTIC LIVING + SIGNIFICANT LIVING = FULL LIVING

An interesting study out of Stanford University was recently published in the Journal of Positive Psychology. The study focused on the how people spend their time and what experiences they cultivate as a result. More specifically, they focused on the similarities and differences between happiness and meaningfulness.

Jennifer Aaker, who headed the study out of the Stanford Graduate School of Business, said that while meaningfulness and happiness overlap, they are distinctly different. *"Happiness was linked to being a taker rather than a giver, whereas meaningfulness went with being a giver rather than a taker,"* Aaker said.

To use our language, her findings suggest that the success resulting from authentic living can reap temporary happiness because it is based upon what you get. But only through living significantly by including the needs of others in our lives — being a giver— can we find meaning.

To further support this, here is a succinct summary of some additional findings of the study as written by Clifton Parker in his Stanford Report article entitled "The Meaningful Life is a Road Worth Traveling":

- <u>Happiness and Meaning:</u> Happiness is achieved when focusing on the present while meaning is the result of thinking about how the past, present, and future relate. Thus, happiness and meaning are the results of different focuses.
- <u>Getting vs Giving:</u> Happiness often results from getting, yet meaning is the result of being able to define yourself and express that authentically — an act that can manifest itself in giving of one's self to a larger purpose in life.

So what does this have to do with living life to the fullest? It provides the perfect summary and affirmation of the core of *TIMEOLOGY*:

<u>Only through gaining perspective on how we trade our time can we live both authentically (realize success and happiness) and significantly (have meaning). And only through living authentically and living significantly are we living life fully.</u>

Success is about getting. So while it can bring about happiness, it is temporary and can be taken away. Even those that have achieved much success in their lives have not found sustained happiness from it — which left them to ask the "then what" questions.

By contrast, significance is about giving. Which means it is perpetual and cannot be taken away. It brings sustained periods of peace, contentment, and meaning because it is part of something bigger than the individual. In fact, this suggests that at the end of life, we will all look back and realize what was truly important, and it won't be things or even the ability to say we had a happy life (though that matters) — it will be relationships and the significance our lives brought to others.

Richard Paul Evans, in *The Five Lessons a Millionaire Taught Me about Life and Wealth* says it this way: "Success in life cannot be measured on a balance sheet. I believe that the truest measure of achievement is the degree to which we've learned to love. And service, through sharing our wealth and our time, is love made visible."

In this way, the math is simple:

<u>Authentic Living + Significant Living = Full Living.</u>

23 THE LEGACY OF SIGNIFICANCE

Let me tell you the story of Ted. Ted was born in the Midwest as one of seven kids. Having so many siblings, he was always around kids and thus, had a natural predisposition to understand the dynamics that led these kids to productive adult lives.

As a productive achiever himself, when Ted grew up and went off to college, he discovered a natural ability and skill in speaking and an interest in legal practice. After finishing his undergraduate degree, he decided to pursue such by going to law school.

Upon graduation, he could have chosen the more lucrative and financially rewarding roles in firms specializing in corporate law, but decided to stay true to his interests and passions for kids. He saw a significant need in that area and thus, he joined a firm with a specialization in adoption, foster parent and dependency litigation, and guardianships.

Over the next 30 years, Ted would help with placing kids for adoptions, advocating for kids in need of permanent and stable homes, and eventually start his own practice dedicated specifically to those needs on which he felt the most called.

But what makes Ted's story so profound, is the way he viewed it. You see, the reason I know Ted's story is because he told it to me when we were adopting our son Hunter.

Paraphrasing, Ted told me, "Matt, as a man of faith, I feel that the evil one puts chaos and hurt into the world through things like unplanned pregnancies, the premature death of parents, rape, and so forth. Almost as if the evil one is saying, 'Ted, what are you going to do about that?' "

Ted paused, then turned back and looked me square in the eye and said, "I'll tell you what I am going to do about that."

"I'm going to start a law office focused on serving the needs of these children. I'll find good families to raise and love these kids. I'll care for and support the needs of the families that had the courage to give them up for adoption. And in so doing, I will change the trajectory of that kid's life. And that kid will have kids that they will raise, and grandkids, and so on. And 100 years from now, long after I am gone, the impact of our work will be felt by tens of thousands who are productive members of society because of what we did here today. And the world will be a better place."

I sat in my chair completely speechless (which for me is saying something since I love to talk). Ted not only had clarity around the significance he had in this process, but in so sharing, gave my wife and me an enlarged perspective on the significance that we were going to have in the life of our son as well. He helped us realize we were part of something even bigger than we thought, and the sense of meaning, peace, contentment, and joy that followed were overwhelming (and still are). I can only imagine the feelings Ted must experience knowing that he has been a catalyst for this type of outcome in the lives of so many children and families.

Ted is a shining example of someone who is living with significance — achieving his dreams and aspirations (to make the world a better place), by pursuing his interests and passions (in children), using his skills and talents (in the practice of law), for the needs of others (children who need a "forever family" and the birth families who need the support and courage to make such hard decisions).

Aside from Ted's story being a great example of someone living with significance, it also exemplifies another important point — that living significantly today, no matter how seemingly small, changes the trajectory of your life, and many others. And it gets multiplied over the passage of time.

Because Ted traded his time in life for significance with his adoption practice, children's lives were impacted positively. Because of that positive impact with the kids, it's likely many will have stronger foundations and positive outlooks on life from which to become productive and positive members of society. The trajectory of their lives was changed in an upward direction. Even if only slightly — say, just a few degrees (to use a geometry illustration) — over time, look at the legacy impact of that significant act that was conducted today:

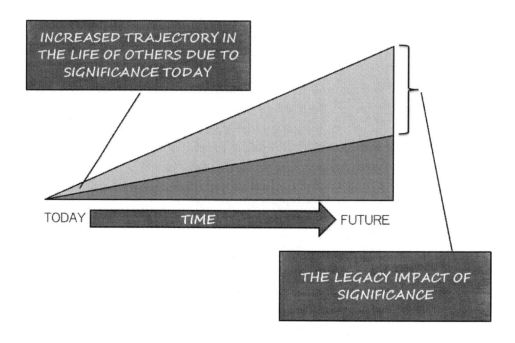

INCREASED TRAJECTORY IN THE LIFE OF OTHERS DUE TO SIGNIFICANCE TODAY

TODAY

TIME

FUTURE

THE LEGACY IMPACT OF SIGNIFICANCE

Furthermore, because these kids saw the impact of others taking the time to invest in their lives, they are more likely to make that part of their lives, perpetuating the situation or "paying it forward".

The point is that living significantly today, no matter how seemingly small, changes the course of lives — the one you are helping and your own. This, when multiplied with the passage of time, creates significance of epic proportion. And the results of that significance are peace, joy, contentment and meaning for those who are catalysts for it — especially when we are lucky enough (have enough perspective) to build it into the vocations of our lives as Ted has.

It is worth pointing out that Ted lives this out beyond his practice. He and his wife have a number of biological children but have also adopted additional children and are living out this significance in their personal family life, just as in their legal practice.

Harkening back to Simon Sinek's "Start with Why" language and model, I would illustrate it this way:

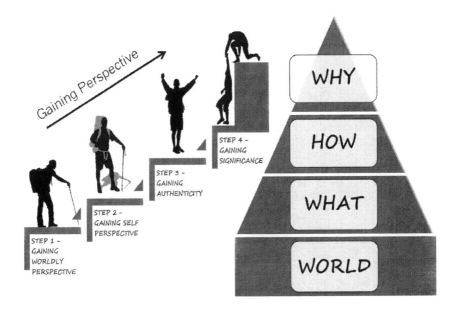

- Through gaining perspective — which he did well before the ideas of this book were formed — Ted has climbed to clarity on his WHY statement in life which, using my words, may go something like this: to create the necessary support and structure so that all children can have the opportunity to live life to the fullest. This makes for significant living in Ted's life.

- Authenticity for Ted is making sure that the WHAT of his life — being a dad, husband, attorney, church member, etc, etc — are in alignment with his WHY. And in Ted's case, it seems he is living authentically across all of these roles.

Yet, not all of us are. And here is how the differences may look between when we are in alignment and out of alignment.

163

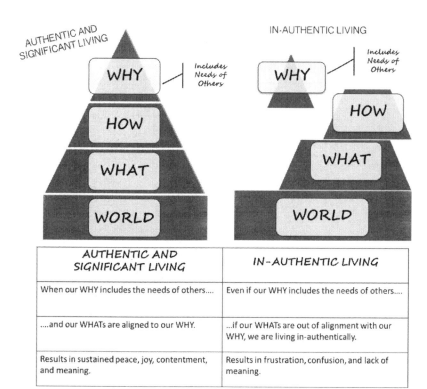

AUTHENTIC AND SIGNIFICANT LIVING	IN-AUTHENTIC LIVING
When our WHY includes the needs of others....	Even if our WHY includes the needs of others....
....and our WHATs are aligned to our WHY.	...if our WHATs are out of alignment with our WHY, we are living in-authentically.
Results in sustained peace, joy, contentment, and meaning.	Results in frustration, confusion, and lack of meaning.

If we are living in-authentically, the fix is to gain PERSPECTIVE. Just pull out the four steps and assess:

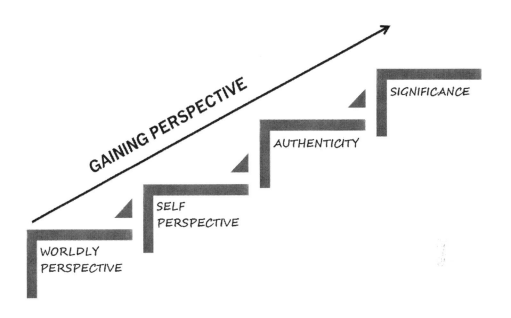

A. <u>Worldly Perspective</u> — What are the roles you are currently filling in the world? (These are your WHATs)

B. <u>Self-Perspective</u> — Get back in touch with your Dreams/Aspirations, Skills/Talents, Interests/Passions. Also, get clarity on the gaps between your Exposé (Who you are) and Epitaph (Who you want to be).

C. <u>Authenticity</u> — Using your Self-Perspective and Worldly Perspective, determine where you are living inauthentically. List the things you are spending your time on versus the things you would like to be spending your time on. Then determine which are out of balance and use the power of habits/routines to make the changes. Said a different way, which of your WHATs are misaligned with your WHY and thus need to go? Which new WHATs could you adopt to be more congruent with your WHY?

D. <u>Significance</u> — Does your WHY include the needs of others? If so, your WHATs will include them too. If not, seek clarity and then be ready to take on opportunities for such as they present themselves.

Let me offer further encouragement to you by sharing another story.

I once heard a speaker tell of a talented and accomplished marketing executive that had led countless successful marketing campaigns for numerous companies throughout corporate America. Aside from being talented in this field, they were passionate about marketing — specifically the opportunity to share and communicate the value proposition of a product or service to the consumer.

But over time, they felt that doing it solely "for profit" left them with the temporary happiness often affiliated with success. They desired something that had more impact, more meaning.

In addition to marketing, this individual was passionate about service men and women who had fought for America's armed forces. More specifically, they were passionate about the children of these service men and women who had lost a father or mother in the line of duty.

So this individual started to trade out one day a week from the "for-profit" business to volunteer on marketing campaigns for a "nonprofit" organization whose mission was to serve these children. This marketer, through using their skills and talents, helped raise the donations and contributions by more effectively getting the word out about the work the organization was doing.

In so doing, the organization's ability to meet this need in the world was raised. Simultaneously, this individual gained joy and peace. They gained significance.

This was the result of finding an opportunity in life that allowed them to utilize their skills and talents and interests and passions for the benefit of others.

So is this epic significance on the same scale as Ted's? Is there such a thing as something that is "more significant" than another?

I would offer that all significance is epic. Let me share my thinking on why.

As Ted taught us, when a single person lives significantly, those who benefit are more likely to "pay it forward" in their own lives. The graphic entitled "Example A" illustrates this. By making a significant act today, the impact of significance goes from the dark area to the completely shaded area. When multiplied by the passage of time, this creates an epic level of significance. Look at the number of lives it impacts! This is the power you wield as a single person who chooses to act significantly in your life!

Which raises the question — what type of change could we accomplish in the world if we could create a movement around living significantly? What if we, as a society, got intentional about finding authentic ways to weave the needs of others into our lives? What could be the impact then?

The answer is it could change the world.

In fact, it would operationalize the famous quote by Mahatma Gandhi: "You must be the change you wish to see in the world." Take a look at "Example B" in the same graphic.

Example A:
The impact of a single person living significantly.

Increased Trajectory in the Life of Others due to Significance Today

Example B
The impact of a movement with numerous people living significantly.

| 25 Years from Now | 50 Years from Now | 75 Years from Now | 100 Years from Now |

By creating a movement with numerous people living significantly, our impact is exponential. Not only do we eventually have an ability to impact everyone in those future generations due to the power of the passage of time, but notice the overlap that starts to occur which illustrates the strength of the movement. People will not only experience the care of one, but the care of many. The message — their lives will feel important. In turn, they will have the courage and support to live their lives to the fullest. Then triangles of significance will permeate from their own lives which is how significance can build and perpetuate an epic legacy.

Perhaps Margaret Mead said it best: "Never doubt that a small group of thoughtful committed citizens can change the world; indeed, it's the only thing that ever has."

24 THE POWER OF PERSPECTIVE

One of the courses I teach at the university focuses on the valuation of corporations or business entities. In the course, I teach seven different valuation models that can be used to offer an opinion of what a company is worth. Since many of our assumptions in business settings are that maximizing shareholder value is the main objective (at least for publicly traded companies), learning how to assess and select actions that maximize the value of the firm is key to training students to be effective managers in the firm. Our students, and those in business schools all around, become very adept at identifying the ways in which firm value is maximized. After all, this represents success, right?

Yet there are many, I being one, who believe that there is more to the existence of a corporation than simply maximizing shareholder value (i.e. making money). In fact, just this week there was yet another example of that playing out in the news.

In their quarterly earnings call with analysts, Costco's CFO Richard Galanti was asked by an analyst "What is your philosophy on chickens?"

The question was in reference to the fact that Costco had not raised the price on their cooked rotisserie chickens in a considerable number of years. Analysts were prodding Costco, who sold approximately 76 million chickens in the previous year, to increase the price just $1.00 due to the significant positive impact it would have on the profitability of the firm.

Galanti's response was classic Costco: "I can only tell you what history has shown us: When others were raising their chicken prices from $4.99 to $5.99, we were willing to eat, if you will, $30 million to $40 million a year in gross margin by keeping it at $4.99. That's what we do..."

In fact, in a similar call a few years earlier, Galanti gave what equated to the same response for staying at the $4.99 price point saying, "That's us. That's what we do."

So while their strategy definitely has elements of increasing food traffic which benefits sales of other products in their stores, Costco sees itself as an organization that provides value in more ways than just financially to their stakeholders – which include not only their shareholders, but also their employees and their customers.

This reminded me of a quote from Peter E. Drucker, often referred to as the "founder of modern management," in his book entitled *Management: Tasks, Responsibilities and Practices*:

"It is the customer who determines what a business is. It is the customer alone whose willingness to pay for a good or for a service converts economic resources into wealth, things into goods. What the business thinks it produces is not of first importance ... What the customer thinks he is buying, what he considers value, is decisive — it determines what a business is, what it produces, and whether it will prosper... The customer is the foundation of a business and keeps it in existence. He alone gives employment. To supply the wants and needs of a consumer, society entrusts wealth-producing resources to the business enterprise."

So what? What does this have to do with perspective? And what does it have to do with living life to the fullest?

Call me a dreamer, but I believe the implications of gaining perspective in our individual lives can have exponential significance on the world, when aggregated. Here's why:

Consider some of the greatest challenges facing humanity today. Global poverty and hunger, water shortages, defeating terrorism without turning the world into a surveillance state, disease, immorality, the education gap, access to medical care, lack of leadership, and countless others. These represent opportunities for us to live both authentically (successfully addressing these challenges) and significantly (because it will simultaneously make a difference for others). Note: this harkens back to the things we would "change about the world."

Since most of us as adults must work for a living, we spend a considerable amount of our time acting in capacities as employees or entrepreneurs. Simultaneously, to meet our basic needs and optional wants, we also act as consumers.

If history is any indicator, corporations and organizations are one of the most powerful platforms from which to create and impact change due to their collective resources and global reach. These entities are a collection of both constituent groups. They have individuals acting as employees — each with our own desire to live authentically and significantly. Simultaneously, they have consumers or customers — each with our own desire to consume their goods or services to meet basic needs or optional wants.

In short, this means we — as both a consumer and as an employee/entrepreneur — wield tremendous power over corporations and organizations.

Allow me to illustrate just one way the power of perspective, when aggregated, can change the world. For good measure, let's weave in the very real demographic shifts facing the world today — the population shift of baby boomers.

While they are retiring at the pace of approximately 10,000 per day, baby boomers, those born between 1946 and 1964, still occupy the executive positions of many organizations with great reach and resource to address the needs of the world.

What if the baby boomers, using those positions of leadership, put their organizations through the process of gaining perspective just as we have done as individuals?   Perhaps it would look something like this.

In worldly perspective, the business would first identify what they are currently doing in the world (the goods and services they are currently offering and to whom). Additionally, instead of identifying their fears, they might instead identify the market threats.   Finally, they would answer the same question we did which is "what would they like to change about the world if they could?"   This would help them identify which of the great challenges or global opportunities they may want to tie off to.

In self-perspective, the organization would memorialize who they truly are. Instead of Dreams and Aspirations, the business would clearly state its Vision and Mission (which many do). Instead of Skills and Talents, the business would articulate their core competencies. Instead of Interests and Passions, the business would state where they desire to carry out the purpose of their work (which could be the sector, industry, and/or markets for focus).   In other words, they can articulate who they are today and who they want to be (a la the exposé and epitaph).

Having achieved worldly perspective and self-perspective, the business could see if it is operating authentically (i.e. achieving success).   Are they using their core competencies, to meet opportunities in their desired markets, to carry out their vision and mission authentically?   When the answer is yes, the results are often rendered in the form of financial success from authentically meeting the needs in the market.

Unfortunately, many corporations — who do most all of the steps I articulated above as part of their strategic planning process — stop at this step of attaining authenticity. After all, they have achieved success. Simply making a profit is enough for them. Their shareholders are happy. They don't see the possible bigger implications of moving to significance with their business. They stop short of asking if their corporation is making a difference that will last. And perhaps they stop short of asking this for the same reasons we often do as individuals — that we think the end we are seeking is what we get, not what we give.

Yet it is this final step of gaining perspective — significance through including the needs of others — which I believe will make *the* difference in the relevance of these organizations (and therefore their ability to make an impact) going forward. Both employees and consumers are not inspired by making the "faceless" shareholder more money. They are inspired by being part of an organization that is significant. By being part of an organization with meaning. By being a part of something that is bigger than what they could accomplish by themselves. In other words, they are looking to find a corporation or organization whose perspective lines up with their own.

In fact, when it comes to gaining perspective, here is a chart that shows how the questions facing us as individuals line up with the questions facing organizations. As employees or consumers, we are looking for corporations who's answers are extensions of our answers as individuals — giving us the opportunity to participate in something authentic and significant to us but on a greater scale.

	INDIVIDUAL	CORPORATION / ORGANIZATION
WORLDLY PERSPECTIVE	What roles are you playing?	What is your product and service offering?
	What are your fears?	What are the threats?
	What would you like to change about the world?	What would you like to change about the world?
SELF PERSPECTIVE	What are your Dreams and Aspirations?	What is your Vision and Mission?
	What are your Skills and Talents?	What are your Core Competencies?
	What are your Interests and Passions?	Which sector, industry, or market do you desire to carry out your purpose?
	Who are you today (Expose) and who do you want to be (Epitaph)?	What are you currently (Expose) and what do you want to be (Epitaph)?
AUTHENTICITY	Are you living authentically? (ie. Are you happy?)	Are you operating authentically? (ie. Is the financial success enough to keep operating?)
SIGNIFICANCE	Are you living significantly? (ie. Do you feel the peace, joy, and contentment that comes from having meaning in your life?)	Are you including the needs of others in why you exist? By so doing, are you making a difference that your employees and consumers can participate in (rather than just hitting quarterly profit goals)?

As you can tell, I feel strongly about this. The reason ties directly to my experiences with students at the university.

One of the biggest challenges I see in mentoring students getting ready to graduate is assisting them in tying off their clarity of perspective with the right job opportunity where it will be complementary and valued. These students are passionate. They are hungry. They desire to get started and make a difference. And while sometimes such eagerness can come off as youthful exuberance, it is exciting to see their desire to "hit the real world running."

Yet even if a student achieves clarity of perspective for themselves, they often have a hard time identifying organizations or corporations which have objectives that resonate with their own. (That is why mentoring and internships are so important and valuable for them.) After all, if they are going to spend 40, 50, 60 or more hours a week in their vocation to provide for their basic needs and optional wants, it is critical that they find something that allows them to pursue both authentic success and significant meaning if they want to experience life to the fullest.

Yet organizations are often vague about or fail to address in any manner how the work they are offering ties off to significance or higher meaning. So vague in fact, that according to the Millennial Survey performed by Deloitte for 2015, over 75 percent of millennials believe businesses are focused on their own agendas rather than helping to improve society. Meaning, they have a perception that most businesses are primarily interested in success with little regard for significance.

But helping society — "having significance" to use our terminology — is something that is important to millennials as both employees and consumers. As a result, many of my students who have gained perspective scanned the marketplace for a business where they could put their interests and passions, skills and talents to work to pursue their dreams and aspirations as well as help others along the way.

Unfortunately, many come up empty handed feeling that the market did not offer an organization with such an opportunity (or at least did not articulate it in such a way that it was visible or transparent).

As a result, some formed new entrepreneurial enterprises which, for my part, offers me optimism about the impact that can be made toward some of these global challenges as the years pass and these companies pick up talent, resources, and momentum. Unfortunately, some other students compromised and went to work for the "best of what was available" which I understand but am saddened by.

But there is another way. Following my example through, by baby boomer leaders helping their organizations gain perspective, it would allow them to achieve a more authentic relationship with their constituent groups (employees and customers) while simultaneously having a story of significance to share in tackling some of the bigger plights of the world. This would provide the organization additional methods of articulating its value to the world beyond simply the financial results that it provides to its shareholder. As organizations became more adept at articulating their value beyond finances, they would attract more talented employees and more customers who want to be a part of something bigger than themselves (like the millennials). After all, it is very hard for one individual to feel like they are making any significant difference on global challenges like poverty or disease or hunger. Yet, by aligning with others making up an organization, the individual achieves the vehicle by which they can make a difference. And the result is everyone wins.

Baby boomers, who may be approaching the end of their career, can find great personal significance by leading their organizations to clarity on communicating value beyond finances. In essence, they could be the catalysts that start changing the trajectory of the world in a positive way on one or more key global challenges. By doing so, they not only address global needs, but catch the attention of the younger millennials and Generation X/Y who are interested in putting their time in the workplace into something more meaningful. As a result, these corporations get more talented employees who can offer their human capital to furthering the cause and carrying the flag forward.

Additionally, it brings multiple generations side by side. It gives the opportunity for those who are younger in life experience to have a forum to hear and learn from those with more life experience and, frankly, vice versa. It gives baby boomers the opportunity to adapt and learn from the perspective of a millennial generation that experienced 9/11, the war on terrorism, the financial crisis, and the global deployment of technology all during their formative years.

And in case you are thinking this is just pie-in-the-sky dreaming on my part, let me share how I have experienced this personally in my own life.

As you know by now, I currently work two full time jobs — one in industry (CFO) and one in academia (professor). This was only possible because a baby boomer, who is my boss in my industry job, felt it important to make enough space in my schedule to allow me to pursue the opportunity to teach at the university. It is worth noting that it would have been easier for him and more cost effective for the organization not to have provided me the opportunity. But he did anyway.

The result?

I have more loyalty and respect for my boss and the corporation than I ever could have from getting a larger paycheck (which underscores the point that we cannot buy the feelings we seek in life but rather they come from enabling the opportunities to live our lives to the fullest). As a result, despite being out of the office a few days a week so I can be on campus, I am more committed than ever to the success of the organization. Finally, to cap it off, it has created more opportunity for others in the organization to move up, take on more responsibility, and continue to live their life to the fullest on their career front.

Simultaneously, through my work in the classroom, which was enabled by the support of my boss in industry, they are vicarious participants. In other words, my boss and the organization are making an investment in the classroom through their support and flexibility for me to be there.

In this way, they provide an excellent example of an organization who is both authentic (successfully serving the residential real estate market by participating in building homes and communities) and significant (giving back by actively investing in the education of those who make up that community).

So, in conclusion, the power of gaining perspective is in the clarity it provides you. Clarity on what it means to live authentic to who you are. Clarity on identifying opportunities to find significance through including the lives of others in what you do.

Only through this clarity can you make the day-to-day decisions consistent with living your life to the fullest.

And that will be the challenge. To use that perspective to make decisions that allow you to remain authentic to yourself while finding significance in the various roles you play in life (in family, in career, in church, in community, etc).

Gaining perspective is the key to living it. Only once you have gained perspective can you utilize all of the other wisdom and subject matter expertise of thought leaders, authors, mentors, family, friends and so forth to maximize your living of life to the fullest. Only then will you have the context of perspective from which to differentiate what is authentically you and significant to you.

So whether you are a student, young adult, someone well into your career and raising family years like I am, a baby boomer, a member of the greatest generation, or anything in between, my question for you is simple: will you gain perspective now so you can live your life to the fullest?

25 IS THIS IT? OR IS THERE MORE?

Up to this point, the book has been about offering a framework for finding authenticity and significance in your life through gaining perspective on who you are and what living life to the fullest looks like for you.   I have tried very hard as your author to share it in a way that removes any biases or beliefs I may have so that you, as my reader, can use the framework freely and without external influence.

That said, woven into that approach has also been the desire to share all of the elements of the framework that are important for gaining a comprehensive perspective from which to live life to the fullest.   And I would not be holding up that end of the bargain if I did not offer you this one last — and perhaps most important — question relating to your perspective.

<u>Is this life it or is there more?</u>

Let me set the context with a lesson from history.

There exist multiple accounts of the life of a man who lived long ago.   He was born in a little known village to parents of humble resources. As a boy, he was naturally curious and enjoyed interacting with those older than he. You might equate him to what we would call an "old soul".

Until he was thirty, he worked in the family business doing manual labor. He did not write any books. He did not hold public office. He did not own a home or livestock or anything of significant material value. He never traveled more than a few hundred miles from where he was born. Yet this humble and unassuming life was very authentic to who he was. And that authenticity proved to be an important launching pad for the impact his life would have in the years to come.

With great clarity about what living his life to the fullest looked like — which focused on helping others — in his early thirties, he started to live out this purpose more intentionally and publicly.

He was a great storyteller and used this gift to teach people life lessons that led them to focus on the things that matter most in their lives. He started speaking out against some of the immoral behaviors, traditions and societal norms of the day. He started to call out those in positions of power for their hypocritical and oppressive ways. Yet because he was so authentic, they could find no faults with the way he lived his life — which made his critique of their lives even more poignant (and irritating to those leaders). It simultaneously made his message more impactful to his audience.

As a result, his influence quickly grew. He gained a following, including a select handful of very close friends who, inspired by his vision and message, left their ways of life to follow the one he spoke of.

This man's rhetoric was so anti-establishment yet so profound that it resonated with the people of the day. He spoke of a higher being that loved each of them and that there was immense value in each and every one of their lives. He spoke of a higher being who would grant them forgiveness for their shortcomings for those who simply asked. And, perhaps most significantly, he spoke of eternal life promised by this higher being for those who believed in the message he shared.

Seeing the destabilizing impact to their "status quo," the leaders of the day felt threatened. As a result, they arrested him, had him tried, sentenced him to death, and executed him on a cross. And in so doing, they put an exclamation point on the life of this one man which was so significant, that some 2,000 years later, billions on the planet today still talk about and follow the example of it.

For my part, as a believer in the life, teachings, death, and eternal promise of Jesus, I would be most simply classified as a Christian. But I share this story with you not to push any religious beliefs onto you. Rather, I share it to make a number of key points that relate back to our efforts to gain perspective so we can live life to the fullest. The points are these:

- That out of any situation, great significance can come.

- That the promise of eternal life offered by Jesus is the only thing I have found in life that I can GET that cannot be TAKEN AWAY.

- That the belief in eternal life offers me the courage and freedom to aggressively pursue living this life to the fullest.

Allow me to elaborate on each.

First, there is an interesting lesson here — that out of humble beginnings and a quiet unassuming life, great significance came. Often times, we may think that we are "too late" to have meaning in our lives or make an impact. Or, we don't have the "means" or the "platform" to have significance. Yet, irrespective of whether you believe in Jesus' teachings and promise of eternal life or not, there is no debating the fact that he has been significant for the last 2,000 years resulting largely from just the last three years of his life. Translation, you can have great significance starting at any time in your life. It is never too late. And it is never limited by your means or lack of a formal platform.

Second, earlier in the book, we illustrated that the things we get — the fruits of success — can be taken away which is why it is important to focus on what we give (significance). But I have found one exception to that rule. I have found one thing that I can get that cannot be taken away — the promise of eternal life in my faith as a Christian.

Because of his sacrifice on the cross, Christians, like me, believe that by believing in Jesus, we will enjoy eternity in heaven with our creator. But what makes this promise extraordinary, is that I don't have to give anything back in order to get it. I don't have to do anything to be able to accomplish it. It is simply a gift for believing in him. The only gift I have ever found that cannot be taken away. And that's what makes it so unique and different from anything else. It's also what makes it so powerful in my life.

Which leads me back to the question you must answer for your own life: <u>Is this life all there is or is there more?</u> You see, whether you answer yes, there is more or no, there is not more, the answer is a key part of your perspective. Let me illustrate how my answer to that question mattered in one of the most challenging times of my life.

It was 3:15 a.m. on a Wednesday morning in August and my home phone rang. Since we live in a cell phone era, it was rare that anyone would call my home phone to begin with, let alone at that time of the morning. I knew it was not good, picked up the phone, and received confirmation of such.

My brother, who by chance had decided to stay at my parents' house that night, said that our dad had just had a heart attack and they were trying to revive him.

I told my brother I was on my way — my parents' house was about 25 minutes away — and for him to call me on my cell phone when they started toward the hospital.

I got to the hospital around 3:40 AM, a few minutes before the ambulance carrying my dad arrived. He was still unconscious and only had what is called a junctional heart rhythm. Despite four passes with the defibrillator, they could not get him back.

As they took my dad out of the ambulance — his head swaying lifelessly back and forth as they changed directions while racing into the ER — my mom and brother arrived and we ran inside.

About 10 feet from where six ER technicians and doctors were frantically working on my dad, it looked like a scene out of a medical TV drama. At this point, it was approaching 3:50 AM and, knowing my dad had been down since approx. 3:15 AM, I figured it would only be a moment or two before someone came over to the three of us and stated, "I'm sorry, there is nothing more we can do."

Miraculously, on what seemed to me like it would be their last attempt, the defibrillator worked and brought back a sustained heartbeat. They immediately induced a medical coma and lowered his body temperature as their concerns quickly turned to the fact that he had been without blood flow to his body for between 35 and 40 minutes — a fact they were indicating likely meant he was brain dead. In fact, it had a name: "clinical death". It's the medical term for when you stop blood circulation and breathing. Research suggests that full recovery of the brain after a period of more than 3 minutes of clinical death at normal body temperature is rare. My dad had approximately 35 to 40 minutes.

As the minutes turned to hours, I sat in the critical care waiting room thinking about my dad's life, my life, and our life together while his fate hung in the balance. It seems that in situations of life and death, our perspective is always challenged and revealed.

While we had had countless amazing and happy times together – my dad was my hero growing up – the things I was most grateful for in that moment were the conversations about life, the lessons he had imparted, and the overall meaning he had in my life. I think it's because I knew that if he didn't make it through, while we would not have any new memories together, I would be able to keep all of the meaning he had already had in my life even after he was gone. What he had done for others — in this case me — was permanent. I could keep the significance his life had had in mine. And as a result, I, as his son, did not have any regrets about our life together. That was comforting.

But what was overwhelming was the prospect of not having his physical presence in my life. As I sat there facing all of the possibilities of what life would be like without him there — he would never meet the rest of his grandchildren, would only have seen me be a dad for one year, and so forth — that was the part that was the most daunting.

Which leads back to the question at hand: Is this life all there is or is there more?

Because I believe in eternal life, if my dad were to die, it is my belief that we would be together again one day in heaven. That offered a different perspective from which to deal and comprehend the situation. In this case, it comforted me. It provided a view on the situation that no matter what happened, it was not the end. It may be the end on Earth, but not the ultimate end.

Which leads to my third and final point — one that added one last dimension to my perspective. As you may or may not know, at the heart of Christianity is the promise of living life to the fullest. In fact, Jesus boldly proclaimed it in the Bible in John 10:10 when he said: *"The thief comes only to steal and kill and destroy; I have come that they may have life, and have it to the full."*

Seriously? He came to offer me the chance to live life to the fullest? Yes, and what a promise!

184

If eternity is already secured in heaven, and it cannot be taken away, it takes the pressure off. When I am fearful of being able to pursue authenticity in my life (because it's hard or counter cultural or is not the choice with the best short term feelings attached), I can move forward with courage anyhow because the real important stuff — where I will spend forever — is already addressed. When I face those life events that are out of my control like the death of loved ones or health issues or whatever, while keeping perspective can help, the real important stuff — where I will spend forever — is already addressed. In summary, it is greatly liberating and comforting in this life to know that through faith, I have one thing that I can get that cannot be taken away. And the by-product is the freedom to live this life to the fullest (and an example of how to do it by living authentically and significantly like Jesus).

In case you were wondering, despite the odds being stacked against him, my dad survived that morning and, five days later, was released from the hospital in route to making a full recovery. Some would call it a miracle. Some would call is just the amazing reach of modern medicine. But perhaps the neurologist on duty that Wednesday morning when my dad arrived at the ER summed it up best.

On the day dad was leaving the hospital, the neurologist asked to join us in the hospital room and just stand like a wall-flower for about 20 minutes passively taking in our conversations.

We, in great gratitude for the work he and so many others had done, said sure, but why?

He answered, "Because in 30 years of practicing medicine, I have never seen a situation like this turn out this way, and I just want to take it all in."

Is this life all there is or is there more? Your answer will be the final determining factor in your perspective.

26 GAINING PERSPECTIVE AND LIVING YOUR LIFE TO THE FULLEST

I desire to have and keep the clarity in my life that Ted, our adoption attorney, has in his. I desire to live in a way that is authentic to who I really am. I desire to find meaning, joy, peace, and contentment by meeting the needs of others through what I trade my time for. In other words, I desire to live my life to the fullest.

But life is lived in the day to day where we must make decisions about the opportunities that we are presented with.

If we are a student, how do we determine what field of study to pursue? How do we figure out if that internship is the right one for us? How do we know if the job offer is the right one to take? How do we know when we have done enough studying?

In life, how do we know if we should keep dating that person? How do we know if we want to have kids? How do we determine whether we need faith in our lives? How do we ensure we make time for the people that are important? How do we balance work

and family? How do we save enough while still living for today?
How do we determine whether to go to this event or that event?
How do we determine when to retire? How should we figure out
what to do to live fully alive?

The questions are endless. And there is no textbook for life that
contains the answers. So how do you answer them? How do you
determine the right decisions to make on a day to day basis to lead
you to living life to the fullest?

The answer, of course, is to utilize your gained perspective.

So, one more time, what are those four steps to gaining
perspective? And what are the key items you need to know for
each?

THE FOUR STEPS TO GAINING PERSPECTIVE

STEP 1 - GAINING WORLDLY PERSPECTIVE

STEP 2 - GAINING SELF PERSPECTIVE

STEP 3 - GAINING AUTHENTICITY

STEP 4 - GAINING SIGNIFICANCE

First, use your worldly perspective. The world is where you live
life; it's your field of play. If you don't choose the opportunities

you desire, life will dictate them for you. Thus, you must know the roles you play in life so you will be able to ensure they are authentic. Assess the roles you play. In short, you are answering the question of "What are you doing with your life right now?"

Second, use your self-perspective. You are unique and there are specific opportunities in the world perfectly suited for you. Knowing who you are and who you want to be is the key to finding them. So, having taken a self-inventory to identify your dreams and aspirations, interests and passions, and skills and talents, you are able to pursue them in the roles you play. Additionally, use the exposé and epitaph comparison to stay conscious of the gaps between who you are and who you want to be. This will help you answer the question of "Who are you, really?"

Third, live authentically by imposing who you want to be on the world, not the other way around. True success is living a life consistent with who you are. Are you spending your time where you want to be? If not, use the habits/routines to make the necessary changes. Ultimately, the question we are trying to answer asks "Is what you do an authentic representation of who you are?" (i.e. do your WHATs align with your WHY?) If the answer is yes, you are living authentically.

Lastly, live significantly through choosing the opportunities where you are able to include the needs of others in your life. While success can lead to great rewards including temporary happiness, it is the significance our lives bring to others that result in the more permanent feelings of peace, joy, contentment, and meaning we seek. This will happen in the places where you are pursuing your dreams and aspirations, by deploying your interests and passions, and using your skills and talents, to meet the needs of others. In short, we are answering the question "Will what you do last beyond you?"

If it helps, here is Gaining Perspective "At a Glance".

189

GAINING PERSPECTIVE – AT A GLANCE

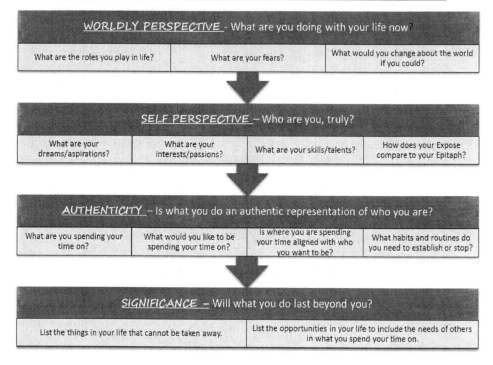

Through gaining perspective, I have found my own why statement — <u>to seek and share knowledge and encouragement so that others can live their life to the fullest.</u>

With this perspective came the realization that some of the things I was doing in my life — my WHATs — were not aligned with this. Over the past handful of years, slowly but surely, I have used my gained perspective and the corresponding tools that accompany it to make the necessary changes in my life.

I stopped doing many things that were out of alignment (myopic focus on finances) and started to do things that were in alignment (more time with my wife, family, teaching, writing, speaking). As a result, when I look at my life now, it is busier than ever but richer than ever in terms of my happiness, joy, contentment, peace, and meaning.

190

My role as husband has new meaning. By being a husband, one of my opportunities in life is to support and encourage my wife living her life to the fullest. This WHAT aligns perfectly with my WHY. I just never saw it that way before.

My role as father to our kids has new meaning. Perhaps the greatest opportunity I have to support another human being living their life to the fullest is through the opportunity to raise them and share life with them. My kids represent the ultimate audience and opportunity for this. Again, another WHAT that aligns perfectly with my WHY. I just never saw it that way before.

How about my career as a CFO? I always prided myself on being a conscientious manager who cared about the people I was responsible for. But now, the view is bigger. I have the chance, through training and empowering them in the workplace, to help them achieve more and support them living their lives to the fullest (even though their careers are only a part of such for them). Yet another WHAT that perfectly aligns with my WHY. I just never saw it that way before.

And I could go on and on.

Perspective has given me a great gift. It has been the view from which I was able to align the things I do to who I really am. And to include the needs of others in what I trade my time for.

In this way, it is the ribbon that has tied together all of the things I do with a higher meaning that, despite doing many of the same things, now renders much more joy and peace and contentment due to it all being interrelated rather than compartmentalized. I can look myself in the mirror and answer the abstract question honestly now. I am living my life to the fullest.

And how do I know?

Because my life is not perfect but now I am okay with that. (A gift of perspective).

Because I am living more authentically today than I did yesterday and have clarity on where I need to go even though I am not there yet. (A gift of perspective).

Because I am not in a perpetual state of happiness and still have ups and downs every day but now I expect them — because happiness is temporary, the result of various successes — and I am okay with that. (A gift of perspective).

Because I have clarity around where I garner meaning in my life and how I can invest in the lives of others. While different from happiness, this significance brings a sense of more perpetual peace, joy, contentment and meaning that alleviates my fear of never having lived. (A gift of perspective).

Ultimately, I know I am living my life to the fullest because now I can see it. The evidence comes from having moved from ?s to !s in my life. Because I have taken the time to gain perspective by answering and continuing to answer the questions necessary to think critically for my life, I can put an ever growing exclamation point on the decisions I make being both authentic and significant. And since Authentic Living + Significant Living = Full Living, I know I am living it.

Will you join me?

MOVING FROM "?" TO "!":
BY GAINING PERSPECTIVE

BY ANSWERING ?'s.....

...YOU LIVE LIFE TO THE FULLEST WITH !

STEP 1 –
GAINING
WORLDLY
PERSPECTIVE

STEP 2 –
GAINING SELF
PERSPECTIVE

STEP 3 –
GAINING
AUTHENTICITY

STEP 4 –
GAINING
SIGNIFICANCE

193

27 KEEPING PERSPECTIVE

Life is a constant journey. You will continue to grow, evolve, and discover more about yourself as you go. Simultaneously the seasons of your life will change. Thus, you cannot be static.

One of the biggest challenges I have encountered with living authentically and living significantly is that it is a constantly moving target. Thus, you must move with it.

Having shared the framework for gaining perspective, I want to offer you a succinct, simple, and practical process for you to keep perspective as you move through your life. Having tried many different things, here is what has worked best in my own journey so far:

1st – Gain Initial Perspective

By reading this book, you have been gaining initial perspective. Especially if you have been doing the activities as you have progressed, you have been doing the necessary critical thinking in your own life. This has likely led you to a number of conclusions about things that you need to change up. (If you have not completed the activities, take some time to go back through the

195

activities and challenge yourself to gain your initial perspective —
taking the time to reduce things to writing in our lives has a great
clarifying effect.)

2nd – Memorialize Your Takeaways

Benefiting from the gained perspective, you need to capture the
handful of takeaway items that you will take action on in the
coming days, weeks, and months to pursue living your life to the
fullest. Below is a simple form that I have used to help me capture
some of the key takeaways. Because gaining perspective is an
additive process with the end goal of living both Authentically and
Significantly, the form focuses on those two outcomes.

LIST THE AREAS YOU LIVE IN-AUTHENTICALLY		KEEPING PERSPECTIVE	LIST THE OPPORTUNITIES TO LIVE SIGNIFICANTLY	
PRIORITY	DESCRIPTION		PRIORITY	DESCRIPTION
1			1	
2			2	
3			3	
4			4	
5			5	
6			6	
7			7	

AREA NEEDING BALANCE / AUTHENTICITY		OPPORTUNITY AREA FOR SIGNIFICANCE	
AREA:		AREA:	
Add or Remove	Routine & Habit	Add or Remove	Routine & Habit
1.		1.	
2.		2.	
3.		3.	
4.		4.	

For authenticity, you need to prioritize the roles you play in life.
You must get clear on which are the priority in this season of your
life. First list all the areas you are living inauthentically (ie. where
you are spending time on things that are not congruent with who
you desire to be). Then, select just one of the most important.

Indicate the Habits and Routines that you will start, and the Habits and Routines you will stop to achieve more authenticity.

For significance, you need to list out all of the opportunities you can think of where you are able to include the needs of others in the things you spend your time on. Then, looking at the list, select one that you are not actively participating in that seems the most exciting and congruent with authenticity in your life. Once you have identified it, select the next steps and habits/routines to start or stop that can allow you to pursue it.

3rd – Conduct a Quarterly Review

In approximately 90 days, circle back and review your takeaways by asking yourself two questions. First, have the habits/routines that you started become an automatic part of your life? Second, have you successfully stopped the habits/routines that were standing in the way?

If the answer is yes to both questions then, congratulations, you have made progress toward living more authentically and living more significantly. If there are other opportunities to address inauthenticity or untapped opportunities for significance you desire to pursue, memorialize them as your next set of takeaways for the next period and follow the same process.

If the answer is no to one or both questions, then assess whether you need more time to make the habits/routines a natural part of your life or if you need to try different ones.

4th – Conduct The "Living Your Life to the Fullest" Tests

As you continue to cycle through the first three parts of this process, you should find your life becoming more authentic and more significant all the time. By weeding out the areas that are inauthentic (and replacing them with authentic habits and routines), as well as pursuing opportunities for significance (by including others in what you do), you will start to feel the benefits you likely sought originally when searching for success and meaning in your life. (Additionally, the clarity you gain on answering questions will make it much easier to make decisions with exclamations.)

Since living life to the fullest is about living authenticity (which leads to periods of happiness) and living significantly (which leads to more perpetual joy, contentment, and meaning), a very simple and logical way to assess whether you are living life to the fullest is simply to ask yourself these two questions.

Question #1 — "Are you happy?"

If you are happy or find the frequency with which you are finding happiness in your life increasing, chances are you are achieving more and more authenticity in a practical sense. Mahatma Ghandi said it this way: *"Happiness is when what you think, what you say, and what you do are in harmony."* Thus, authenticity in our lives brings about happiness. If the byproduct of finding authenticity is more present in your life, it is logical that you are living more authentically as a result. That said, if you find yourself off course, here is a quick analyzer to help you keep perspective on authentic living.

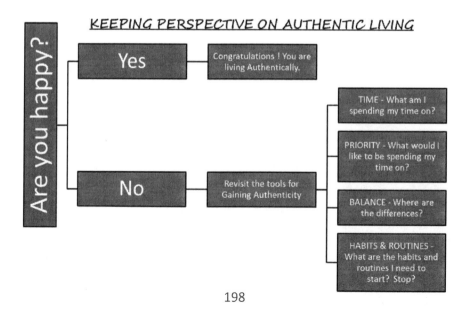

KEEPING PERSPECTIVE ON AUTHENTIC LIVING

Question #2 — "Are you Joyful?"

The second question is simply, "Are you joyful?" Or, said a different way, do you find yourself experiencing more regular and consistent peace and joy from the meaning in your life through serving the needs of others? Since joy, peace, and contentment are the natural byproducts of finding more meaning in our lives, it serves to reason that you have found increased significance in a practical sense. That said, if you find yourself off course, here is a quick analyzer to help you keep perspective on significant living.

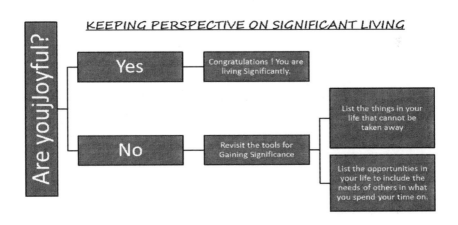

That's it; that's the process for keeping perspective. Just a cycle through the first three parts with an occasional timeout to conduct part four on whether you are living your life to the fullest.

In my experience, while I have toyed with far more detailed processes than these in implementing this in my own life, I have found that going too much deeper just adds administration without value. In other words, at times I had tried to manage through maintaining massive lists of all of the elements that made up my gained perspective. Long lists of all of the interests and passions, skills and talents, dreams and aspirations that I could think of. I tried to continue to keep them updated (which was exhausting). I was regularly reconciling them against where I was spending my time that week versus the week before and so forth. In short, I was TOO CLOSE TO IT. And when that would happen, I would lose perspective. The perspective I had worked so hard to gain and implement in my life.

Thus, my parting encouragement for you is to not over complicate it. Know when enough is enough for you. Don't get stuck in the weeds by trying to administrate the satisfaction of living life to the fullest. Rather, use the gained perspective to focus on the areas that matter. And there are only two: living authentically and living significantly.

Living authentically — true to who you are — is true success. It results in happiness in your life. The more authentic you are, the more happiness you will realize. But keep in mind, it is temporary as it comes from getting.

Living significantly — including the needs of others in what you do in life — is how you create meaning. It results in more perpetual joy, contentment, and peace. And because it's based on what you give, it cannot be taken away.

Only through gaining and keeping perspective will you have a view on what living life to the fullest is for you. Only then will you be able to give names to the things you do in life that are authentic and significant. Truly living life to the fullest will involve a balance of both authentic living and significant living. Only through both can you merge the happiness with the peace, joy, and contentment that you seek.

28 IT'S YOUR TIME

Facing a battle in the epic movie "Braveheart," Mel Gibson's character, William Wallace, gives a speech to his fellow Scotsman who are fighting for freedom from the oppression of the English (who were raping their women, and murdering men, women and children).

The Scottish army, made up of a motley crew who look ill-equipped to challenge the uniformed, groomed, and well-armed English, are assembled in a line — trying to determine whether to fight or run.

Wallace point blank asks his fellow Scotsmen "Will you fight?".

Immediately, a veteran soldier responds "Fight? Against that? No, we will run; and we will live".

It is to this comment that Wallace offers the most pivotal speech in the movie: "Aye, fight and you may die. Run and you'll live — at least a while. And dying in your beds many years from now, would you be willing to trade all the days from this day to that for one chance, just one chance to come back here and tell our enemies that they may take our lives, but they'll never take our freedom?"

You face that same choice. While not staring down the likes of the English army, you do face an enemy and you must make a decision.

Your enemy is inauthentic and insignificant living. An enemy that uses the world in which you live to perpetuate such through its numerous invitations that lead down dead-end paths. An enemy that offers only temporary and limited rewards. An enemy that consumes your most important resource of time and often leaves only regret as the result.

But there is another way.

By gaining perspective, you can conquer your enemy through pursuing authentic and significant living. In so doing, you remove the possibility of regret and replace it with living life to the fullest. You remove the possibility of fleeting happiness and supplement it with joy, contentment, and meaning that cannot be taken away. And on top of it all, you build a legacy by presenting an example and leaving a path for others to find what you have found.

So get going. It's your time; or should I say, TIMEOLOGY!

AFTERWORD

"The Gift of Perspective:

Your First Opportunity for Significance"

AFTERWORD

Let me start by thanking you for the opportunity to share *TIMEOLOGY* and for taking the time to read it. My hope is that the value you received from it was worth the time you invested — and that *TIMEOLOGY* has given you a framework from which to be more effective in trading your time to live your life to the fullest.

As someone who pursues significance from supporting others living their lives to the fullest, I wanted to take a moment to tell you about the other things I am working on to support our mutual journey.

Since life is fundamentally about how we spend our time, I have assembled a website appropriately titled www.ItsAboutTime.life. This can be home base for all of us "Timeologists" looking to trade time for bigger living. (Take a moment to check out the site and add your email to the mailing list. This will ensure we can stay in contact beyond the pages of this book.)

Through blogging on the site, I will continue to share the knowledge, wisdom, and encouragement that I come across in my journey — be it from mentors, thought leaders, or simply experiences from my own life.

This also gives us an opportunity to continue the conversation. Through interaction on these posts, we can stay in contact and sharpen these principles allowing us to encourage one another on the journey to live more fully.

The site will also contain additional resources. From downloadable models and tables from *TIMEOLOGY* to additional tools from other authors and thought leaders, I will endeavor to shine a light on content that will be helpful and encouraging to us all as we continue pursuing full living.

Lastly, the site includes my contact information. If I can be of any direct assistance to you or your organization in gaining perspective and living fully, please reach out. Again, as someone who lives fully by helping others do the same, these represent great opportunities for me to do just that.

With all that said, my final request would be this: if reading this book has helped you gain perspective on ways you can live your life to the fullest, use this as your first opportunity for significance. List five people that you know who would also benefit from *TIMEOLOGY* in their lives…

1. _____
2. _____
3. _____
4. _____
5. _____

…and be the one who gives them that gift.

To living life to the fullest!

Matt

ACKNOWLEDGEMENTS

ACKNOWLEDGEMENTS

So much of what someone can achieve or accomplish in life is due directly or indirectly to the investments of time by others. My life is no exception. As I look back at my life, there have been so many who have traded their time for my benefit. The significance you have had in my life is something I can never fully repay. What I can do is offer this book as a way of acknowledging your significance in my life and paying it forward as an effort to say thank you.

To my wife, Melanie, without you this book simply would not have happened. Thank you for helping create the space in our schedules for me to write it. Thank you for encouraging me to see it through when I didn't think I had anything left to give. Most of all, thank you for being the inspiration for living it. You see, more than anyone else I know, you offer me a daily example of living authentically and living significantly in everything you do. You embody the essence of living life to the fullest. This example and your support of my exploration of all that life has to offer is the reason I feel fully alive. I love doing life with you. But most of all — simply stated — I love you.

To Kaylee, Hunter and Christian, in so many ways, this book is written for you as it fulfills my desire to give you a framework to "figure life out" more quickly than I did. As you get older, I look forward to sharing the meaning you have given my life so you can fully comprehend how amazing a gift you are. For now, despite being only six, four, and two, I want you to know the clarity of purpose you have brought to my life through yours. Mommy and I love you to the moon and back.

To Mom and Dad, thank you for making us kids the focus of your lives. We always felt loved, heard, supported, and encouraged. You were ever-present while striking the challenging balance between exploration and discipline, fun and focus, which you did masterfully. Perhaps the best way I can communicate my gratitude is to say that the standard I desire to achieve for my children has been set by that which I experienced being yours. My life with you has been an amazing gift — one I can never repay. Your lives are — and will always be — the essence of significance in my life. I love you.

To my brother Scott and sister Lindsay, I love you guys and loved the childhood we spent together. I would never trade it, never. Most of all, thank you for always supporting me in the various endeavors on which I spent my time. No matter what, I knew you had my back and still do. And while I wish that we all lived on the same street and our kids all went to the same bus stop to get to school, I am inspired by the people you are, the families you have built with your amazing spouses, and the authenticity with which you live your lives. (Scott, a special thanks for being a sounding board on this book. You are one of only a few people I can rely on for brutally honest feedback in life. That is a gift.)

To my family, thank you for always supporting me and giving me attention for doing the right things in my life, rather than the wrong things. So much of this book, as well as who I have become in life, is because of your investments in me.

Grandma Munson, we have shared so much life together — side by side through births, deaths, celebrations, and trying times. Through it all, you have always been a stabilizing and consistently positive force. You live a life of great significance — and all these years, I have been one of the primary beneficiaries. I am so grateful that you are my grandmother.

Grandpa Munson, thanks for making us grandkids the spring in your step. We felt it. You have been gone for what feels like forever. Yet even after all these years, I still miss going to breakfast with you.

Grandma Giovannoni, thank you for teaching me about life while you taught me to play cards. In many ways, you brought out the teacher in me and embody the importance of education in my life. For that, and so much more, I will always be grateful.

Grandpa Giovannoni, you are my knight in shining armor. Your impact on my life is too significant to try to list here. Perhaps I can sum it up best by saying that one of my greatest honors in life is being your grandson.

Uncle Johnny (MC), what can I say? I love you so much. And of all your traits, the one I appreciate most is the authenticity from which you operate. It has helped me to be bolder in my own authenticity over the years.

Aunt Tracy, you were the first to give me books on finance which helped me discover some of my interests and passions. You have had such a positive and supportive impact on my life, thank you!

To my only first cousin Marcie, I am so proud of you for so many things but most of all, for the courage to chart a life that is authentically your own in Oregon. I miss you, though.

Aunt Weezie, I love our talks and time together. Your perspective always brings something to consider.

Art and Carole, I cherish our times in Art's study at "the ranch". So much wisdom has been shared with me in that forum over the years.

To the Hitts, I always look forward to the times we spend together. Thank you for always taking a positive interest in my life.

To the DeMartinis, if I had one wish growing up it's that we lived closer and could have spent more time together. That said, I cherish so many great memories and have enjoyed seeing the next generation of our family start to grow.

Jim and Julie, you are the best in-laws ever. Thank you for raising such an amazing woman in my wife; what I feel about my parents she feels toward you. And thank you for loving me like a son. Your encouragement and constant support of us gives us the courage to live fully.

Cheryl, Dave, and Jake: you are family. Thank you for being a positive force in my life. You are part of so many amazing memories of living life fully.

To the Schindler, Chao, Buckley, Hogan, Moore, Murphy, McCue, Geronsin, Willardson, Herman, Moses, McMartin, and Weiner families: the memories and impact you have had on my life are too significant to recount here. Whether it was youth sports or neighborhood friendships, virtually every memory growing up involves one of you. Please know I am grateful for your role in my life and especially grateful that so many of those friendships have endured all of these years.

To all of my teachers and professors, coaches and teammates, classmates and colleagues, bosses and mentors, and great friends — the truth is you are too numerous to call out by individual name. The old adage is "It takes a village to raise a child". That resonates for me as I reflect on the investment you all have and continue to make in my life. We often don't know the impact we make on others and perhaps life intends it that way. For my part, please know the gratitude I feel for the time you have spent in your own vocation of life and the benefit I received because of that in mine.

Lastly, I would be remiss if I did not thank the following specific people or groups; without them this book would not have been possible:

Mrs. Plante, for me, it seems life started in your 3rd grade class. It will forever mark the epitome of being fully alive with everything being possible. Thank you for that amazing year and creating an environment of possibility so profound that it still resonates decades later.

Greg, our talks in late high school and early college were some of the most important of my life. While sometimes hard to hear, I appreciate the combination of candor and humor with which you challenged me and gave me feedback. I will forever be grateful and want you to know I miss you. I look forward to giving this book to your girls in your memory.

Gary, you gave me the deal of the century when you offered to share your wisdom in exchange for a $2 cup of coffee as I started my professional career. I will always be grateful for the lessons you shared with me that day and each time we got together. You and your family will forever be an important and treasured part of my life.

Jim, you were the right man at the right time as I entered and explored the "real-world" after graduation. You taught me so much as my boss, but even more as one of my most significant friends. And still do. Thank you.

Yvonne, you are a kindred spirit. Thank you for being such an amazing colleague. I grew and learned so much while working alongside you. More than that, thank you for your gift of friendship. I cherish the lunches and life conversations we had over them. I miss you and Rich and we have a visit to NZ on our "bucket list".

To the team at BAX, I am forever grateful for the opportunity to start my career alongside all of you. While the names are too numerous to share here, I owe a special thanks to Dante, Paul, Rob, Mark, Jeff, Joey, Dennis, Steve, Kevin, John, Rick, Doris, Terry, Dawn and so many others for the opportunities you afforded me so early in my career. And of course, the part I was most proud of, being a member of the GPT. To Gurdip, Nick, Laurent, Eddy, Bob, Sheila, Flora, Tony, Alex, Nuri, Harry, and our Irvine team, I think back with such fondness on being part of this group and long to experience something like it again. But perhaps what made it so special was that it did not last forever.

Bill, thank you for the "real world PhD" you afforded me. You, perhaps as much as anyone, have challenged my thinking and sharpened my perspective.

Tim, thank you for the opportunity and support in pursuing my numerous interests and passions in life. The chance to simultaneously work and teach is a gift I can never repay except to say, thank you.

Steve, the way you think and approach things has broadened my perspective. But the true gift has been your friendship. We are overdue for a hike.

To the Chapman University community and specifically the Argyros School of Business and Economics; in my view, the classroom provides the ultimate platform for living fully as it allows for the pursuit of success while simultaneously investing and sharing the ingredients for such with others. It is an honor to be a part of this institution and participate in the mission to prepare our students to be truly global citizens. A special thanks to my colleagues — many of them mentors and former professors of mine — as well as the administration for the opportunity to participate in that platform in the Argyros School. Additionally, I would like to thank the Chapman50 alumni organization. It is an honor to be a part of a group who has made it their personal mission to live significantly for the benefit of students at the university.

To my GSLC family, it is an amazing gift to have the opportunity to go through life with so many authentic people with great perspective. My perspective has been forever broadened by our shared beliefs and encouraged by the daily example you all set. I am especially grateful for the positive role so many of you have in my life personally. Pastor Hale, thank you for welcoming us and plugging us in. Pastor Mike, you are the shining example of authenticity. Pastor Ryan, your friendship and our life experiences traveling around the world on "outreach" have changed my life. Pastor Tom, thank you for helping me overcome my intellectual battle with perspective (and keeping me in check when needed). Your role in my life has great value and meaning to me and always will.

To the Rancho "Vaquero" clan, I grew up on the green and gold. The examples of marriage, friendship, and values that you represented over the years had far more impact on the perspective of all us "kids" than we will likely ever know (or tell you)! For my part, I am extremely grateful for the friendship you shared with our family all this time. It has offered proof that that type of community is possible.

Finally, I would like to thank Julie for her talents in editing the book. Julie, your giftedness in this arena helped me to ensure the message I was communicating was clear to the reader. Additionally, Kevin, thank you for sharing your experiences to help me navigate the publishing process. Your "perspective" helped me find much needed clarity and expedite the completion of the book. To Ann, thank you for offering me your perspective on my semi-final draft. Your suggestions and affirmations were encouraging at just the right time. Kelly, thank you for your coaching and encouragement – there truly is no time like right now. Lastly, Tom, thank you for consultation and advice on all the legal matters relating to this venture. Your experience and advisement was and remains of great value to me in this ever evolving process and adventure.

APPENDIX

NOTES

PREFACE: Why

1) Simon Sinek, Start with Why, Portfolio 2011, ISBN: 978-1591846444
2) Email April 15, 2015 from Inspireme@StartWithWhy.com from Simon Sinek Inc.

INTRODUCTION

CHAPTER 1 — Living Life to the Fullest

1) John C. Maxwell, The Journey from Success to Significance, Thomas Nelson 2004, ISBN 978-1404101111

CHAPTER 2 — Timeology

1) Quote by Harvey MacKay,
http://www.goodreads.com/quotes/79511-time-is-free-but-it-s-priceless-you-can-t-own-it

2) Quote by Henry David Thoreau,
http://www.brainyquote.com/quotes/quotes/h/henrydavid106427.html

CHAPTER 3 — A Seductive World

1) "Decision Making" by Susan Perry,
http://www.brainfacts.org/Sensing-Thinking-Behaving/Awareness-and-Attention/Articles/2009/Decision-Making
2) Hal Urban, "Life's Greatest Lessons: 20 Things that Matter", Touchstone 20014, ISBN-13: 9780743237826

CHAPTER 4 — Gaining Perspective

1) "The Paradox of Choice",
   http://en.wikipedia.org/wiki/The_Paradox_of_Choice

2) Greg McKeown, Essentialism, 2014 Crown Business, ISBN-13:
   978-0804137386

CHAPTER 5 — Authenticity

1) Define Authentic,
   http://dictionary.reference.com/browse/authentic

CHAPTER 6 — Significance

1) Quote by Martin Luther King, Jr,
   http://en.wikiquote.org/wiki/Martin_Luther_King,_Jr.

CHAPTER 7 — A Call to Action

1) Jim Stovall, "Wisdom of the Ages", Executive Books, 2001, ISBN:
   978-0937539538

PART I: GAINING WORLDLY PERSPECTIVE

CHAPTER 9 — Life's Complicating Factors

1) "US Total Media Ad Spend Inches Up, Pushed by Digital", August
   22, 2013, http://www.emarketer.com/Article/US-Total-Media-Ad-
   Spend-Inches-Up-Pushed-by-Digital/1010154
2) "The Wisdom of John Wooden" by Steve Churm, August 18,
   2005, http://www.ocmetro.com/t-John_Wooden_081805.aspx

CHAPTER 10 — Gaining Your Worldly Perspective

1) Quote by C.S. Lewis, http://www.goodreads.com/quotes/702-it-would-seem-that-our-lord-finds-our-desires-not
2) "You've Got to Find What you Love" Job's Says by Stanford Report, June 14, 2005, http://news.stanford.edu/news/2005/june15/jobs-061505.html

PART II: GAINING SELF PERSPECTIVE

1) "Those Sneaky Agreements" by John Eldredge, January 26, 2009, http://blog.ransomedheart.com/john/2009/01/those-sneaky-agreements.html

CHAPTER 11 — Agreements

1) "Benefits of College Still Outweigh Costs, Fed Study Says" by Katherine Peralta, June 24, 2014, http://www.usnews.com/news/articles/2014/06/24/benefits-of-college-still-outweigh-costs-fed-study-says

CHAPTER 13 — The Exposé and the Epitaph

1) Define Exposé, http://dictionary.reference.com/browse/expose
2) Define Epitaph, http://dictionary.reference.com/browse/epitaph?s=t
3) Quote by J.M. Barrie, http://en.wikiquote.org/wiki/J._M._Barrie

PART III: GAINING AUTHENTICITY

1) Jim Stovall, Wisdom of the Ages, Executive Books, 2001, ISBN: 978-0937539538

CHAPTER 15 — Authentic Living and the Tools to Get You There

1) Quote by Robert Louis Stevenson, http://www.brainyquote.com/quotes/quotes/r/robertloui133527.html

2) On the Shortness of Life by Lucius Annaeus Seneca - http://www.forumromanum.org/literature/seneca_younger/brev_e.html

3) "If I Had to Live it Over Again" by Tony Campolo, http://tonycampolo.org/if-i-had-to-live-it-over-again/#.VWM6R_IVhBc

4) Quote by Thomas Merton, http://www.brainyquote.com/quotes/quotes/t/thomasmert385072.html

5) John C Maxwell, The 15 Invaluable Laws of Growth, Center Street, 2014, ISBN 9781455518227

6) Quote by Aristotle, http://www.brainyquote.com/quotes/quotes/a/aristotle145967.html

7) Darren Hardy, The Compound Effect, 2012 Vanguard Press, 978-1593157241

8) "How Long Does it Actually Take to Form a New Habit? (Backed by Science)" by James Clear, http://jamesclear.com/new-habit

9) "Tale of Two Wolves", http://www.nanticokeindians.org/tale_of_two_wolves.cfm

CHAPTER 16 — Lessons for Authentic Living

1) Quote by Mark Twain, http://www.goodreads.com/quotes/31860-i-ve-lived-through-some-terrible-things-in-my-life-some

2) "Our Concept and Definition of Critical Thinking", The Critical Thinking Community, http://www.criticalthinking.org/pages/our-concept-of-critical-thinking/411

CHAPTER 17 — Then What?

1) "A Statistician's View: What Are Your Chances of Winning the Powerball Lottery?" by Ronald Wasserstein, May 16, 2013, http://www.huffingtonpost.com/ronald-l-wasserstein/chances-of-winning-powerball-lottery_b_3288129.html
2) Define Marginal Utility, http://en.wikipedia.org/wiki/Marginal_utility
3) "Why Lottery Winners Crash After A Big Win" by Robert Pagliarini, September 27, 2013, http://www.forbes.com/sites/robertpagliarini/2013/09/27/why-lottery-winners-crash-after-a-big-win/

PART IV: GAINING SIGNIFICANCE

1) Define Titanic, http://en.wikipedia.org/wiki/RMS_Titanic
2) Define Titanic Passenger List, http://en.wikipedia.org/wiki/RMS_Titanic#Passengers
3) George Strait, I'll Be There, Lyrics, http://lyrics.wikia.com/George_Strait:You%27ll_Be_There

CHAPTER 18 — The Significance of Giving

1) Quote by Albert Pike, http://en.wikiquote.org/wiki/Albert_Pike
2) Quote by Winston Churchill, http://www.brainyquote.com/quotes/quotes/w/winstonchu131192.html
3) Quote by Garth Brooks, http://www.brainyquote.com/quotes/quotes/g/garthbrook382904.html
4) Quote by Albert Einstein, http://www.brainyquote.com/quotes/quotes/a/alberteins145936.html

CHAPTER 19 — No Matter the Size, It's All Significant

1) "Our History", World Vision, http://www.worldvision.org/about-us/our-history
2) "Our Impact", World Vision, http://www.worldvision.org/our-impact
3) Quote by Loren Eiseley, http://www.goodreads.com/author/quotes/56782.Loren_Eiseley

CHAPTER 21 — A Life of Significance

1) Quote by Aristotle, http://www.goodreads.com/quotes/431261-where-your-talents-and-the-needs-of-the-world-cross

CONCLUSION

CHAPTER 22 — Authentic Living + Significance Living = Full Living

1) "The Meaningful Life is a Road Worth Traveling" by Clifton Parker, January 1, 2014, http://news.stanford.edu/news/2014/january/meaningful-happy-life-010114.html
2) Richard Paul Evans, The Five Lessons a Millionaire Taught Me About Life and Wealth, 2006 Touchstone, ISBN 978-0743287005

CHAPTER 23 — Epic — The Legacy of Significance

1) Quote by Mahatma Ganddi, http://www.brainyquote.com/quotes/quotes/m/mahatmagan109075.html
2) Quote by Margaret Mead, http://www.brainyquote.com/quotes/quotes/m/margaretme100502.html#kEVGCkd00LLZIiCY.99

CHAPTER 24 — The Power of Perspective

1) "Why Costco May Never Raise Prices on $4.99 Chickens, $1.50 Hot Dogs" by Brad Tuttle, May 29, 2015, http://www.msn.com/en-us/news/other/why-costco-might-never-raise-prices-on-dollar499-chickens-dollar150-hot-dogs/ar-BBkoy7n

2) Peter E. Drucker, Management: Tasks, Responsibilities, and Practices, page 61,New York: Harper & Row 1973, ISBN 81-8424-148-8

3) "Do 10,000 Baby Boomers Retire Every Day?" by Glenn Kessler, July 24, 2014, http://www.washingtonpost.com/blogs/fact-checker/wp/2014/07/24/do-10000-baby-boomers-retire-every-day/

4) http://www2.deloitte.com/global/en/pages/about-deloitte/articles/millennialsurvey.html

CHAPTER 25 — Is this It or Is There More?

1) "The Millenial Survey 2014", Deloitte, http://en.wikipedia.org/wiki/Clinical_death

2) Bible Passage, https://www.biblegateway.com/passage/?search=John+10:10

CHAPTER 27 — Keeping Perspective

1) Quote by Mahatma Gandhi, http://www.brainyquote.com/quotes/quotes/m/mahatmagan105593.html

CHAPTER 28 — It's Your Time

1) Quote from Braveheart Movie, Paramount Pictures, 1995, http://en.wikiquote.org/wiki/Braveheart

GLOSSARY

As many concepts and terms are introduced and often referred to throughout the book, compiling them into this glossary may be helpful for your ease of reference.

Time: The only truly global currency. Whether rich or poor, old or young, girl or boy, smart or not, tall or short, we only get 24 hours in a day. Our ability to live life is limited by one un-renewable resource: time. We can spend time on an infinite number of paths, choosing our own adventure of life to live out. But choose wisely as we only get one lifetime.

Authentic Living: Being true to who you really are and making decisions and choosing paths in your life consistent with that. Leads to success.

Inauthentic Living: Succumbing to the temptations and fears presented by society resulting in living a life that is not who you really are. Often results in long term regrets.

Success: Achieving or acquiring; it is fundamentally about getting. This can take the form of the things we acquire or gain through trading our time in life including but not limited to financial and material possessions (car, house, boat, jewelry, etc), recognition, fame, power, etc. Usually leads to happiness but, because it's based upon getting, the happiness is temporary.

Significance: By contrast to success, which is about getting, significance is focused on giving. At its core, significance is realized by including the needs of others in our lives. While success can bring temporary feelings of accomplishment or achievement which breed happiness, it lacks permanence. Significance brings about a sense of meaning which results in more perpetual feelings for joy, contentment, and peace which are the ends many of us were ultimately seeking.

Living Life to the Fullest: Only by gaining perspective will we have a view on what living life to the fullest is for us. It will contain both elements of Authentic Living (Happiness) and Significant Living (Meaning). It is through the combination of both that life is lived fully.

Timeology: The gaining of perspective and resulting pursuit of trading our time to live our lives to the fullest. It bridges the gap between the ever-present question of "how we spend our time" and the often abstract desired outcome of "living life to the fullest". By gaining perspective, the two are related in a manner that allows for day to day decision making on how time is spent that aligns with authentic living and meaningful significance for the individual.

Perspective: The ability to see things clearly by having a beneficial vantage point or view on reality. In the context of this book, it is the lessons, wisdom, stories, and overall benefit of experience — both our own and those of others investing in us.

Gaining Perspective: The four step process which leads to living life to the fullest.

- o Gaining Worldly Perspective: "What are you doing with your life now?"

- o Gaining Self Perspective: "Who are you, really?"

- o Gaining Authenticity: "Is what you do an authentic representation of who you are?"

 o Gaining Significance: "Will what you do last beyond you?"

The World: Our field of play for life. The place where our lives get lived out.

Life's Invitations: The competing priorities or aspects of life, inherent in the world, that require time. Oftentimes, they are things representing our basic needs or optional wants.

Life's Complicating Factors: The temptations and fears inherent in the world, that influence our path to authentic living.

Agreements: Conscious or unconscious decisions we have made to accept life and any corresponding consequences and limitations on our life. Norms we have accepted in our life without really thinking them through or asking why.

Dreams and Aspirations: What we envision doing if we were living our highest and best life as we see it.

Interests and Passions: The things that we really enjoy doing in life. We often lose track of time when doing them.

Skills and Talents: The things we do comparatively better than most others.

The Exposé: A short writeup profiling who as person really is. Who we are today.

The Epitaph: A brief writing, following death, of who an individual was. Our "aspired" self. Who we desire to be.

Prioritization: Assigning a level of importance to the various invitations in life.

Balance: Giving time to things commensurate with their true importance, not societal or worldly imposed importance.

Routines and Habits: Tools to assist in creating balance in one's life intentionally.

Opportunities: The chances, in life, to trade our time for an authentic life, fully alive.

Made in the USA
San Bernardino, CA
26 May 2016